DRIVING THE SILK ROAD

DRIVING THE SILK ROAD

Halfway Across the World in a Bentley S1

Douglas McWilliams

First published in 2019
by whitefox

Copyright © Douglas McWilliams, 2019

The author asserts his moral right to be
identified as the author of this work.

Hardback 978-1-912892-71-6
eBook 978-1-912892-72-3

Designed and typeset by seagulls.net
Project management by whitefox
Cover design by James Nunn

Printed and bound by
CPI Group (UK) Ltd, Croydon, CR0 4YY

To Michael, whose mechanical hard work kept us going, and to Ianthe and Rowena, who had to put up with Mike's and my absence and hold the fort at home. And to Mike's and my parents, who take the blame for introducing us to the world and who stood for hours in the blazing sun to welcome us to Paris.

CONTENTS

FOREWORD

I have written this book to say thank you to all those who helped in myriad different ways to make it possible for my brother Mike and I to drive a Bentley S1 from Beijing to Paris in the world's toughest endurance rally. This year's rally has been voted the Motor Sports Event of the Year for 2019, quite an accolade, and we are pretty proud to have been part of it.

I still have to kick myself to realise we not only actually completed the rally but did so entirely under our own steam, not being towed or carried on a flatbed truck on any part of the journey at all. That had always been our objective and we were delighted to achieve it.

It would be wonderful to think that we managed it entirely due to our own efforts. But it wouldn't be true. We had a huge amount of help from other people without whom we would never have completed the rally or indeed got much past the start. And we were also helped by what seemed an undue share of good luck. It often seemed that we had a guardian angel flying above us, providing divine intervention when needed.

Our first thanks go to the rally organisers. It is no easy task to get so many people halfway across the world over diffi-cult terrain. The Endurance Rally Association performed some pretty amazing feats to achieve this and many congratulations are due to them. Obviously they got a few things wrong but it would be silly to focus on the relatively few mistakes they made against their huge achievement in running the rally so well. To Tomas, Patrick, Johnn, Guy and the rest of the team (especially Annette in the office): very well done and many thanks. Their work (and that of us participants) has been recognised in the rally being chosen as the Motor Sports Event of the Year.

Of those on the rally, particular thanks are due to the sweeps, the amazing mechanics who accompanied the rally. They all played a part in fixing broken bits of the car and often had to endure gruelling days and nights with very little sleep while they helped us get to the end. Special thanks are due to Jack Amies, who, having owned a Bentley fairly similar to ours, often managed to mend things when no one else knew what to do. We called upon the sweeps about forty times on the rally and they never said no. So thanks a million to Jack, Alan, Alan, Tony, Andy (Skippy), Rob, Russ and Nicolai.

Four teams of professional local mechanics also did us proud.

In Ulaanbaatar we discovered slightly late in the day that the chassis had started to crack. One of the assistants working for Nomads took Mike to a series of welding shops until they found someone who could do the job. He found an angle iron in his backyard, sawed it down to an appropriate length and welded it to the chassis. It is now a permanent fixture!

In Novosibirsk we discovered that the front suspension and steering had broken. Nicolai, the Russian-speaking sweep, found a shop that might repair the broken parts. It turned out that the driver's side cross pin had sheared in two places, leaving the steering arms dangling. Nicolai's mechanic took the broken part to a local metal worker who turned and threaded a replica part from scratch. This was an impressive bit of engineering.

In Ufa we were sent by Kyrgyz Concept to the local Toyota garage, who had volunteered to help. One of the other cars there was a Datsun 240Z with a mechanic who had been in charge of more than a dozen Paris Dakar rallies. The Bentley had a major refurbishment of the braking system and Mike had the tyres changed. It also returned looking clean, clearly the way that Ufa's Toyotas are returned to their owners.

But most impressive was Nizhny Novgorod. Our brakes had gone and metal was scraping metal – detectable both by sound and smell. Kyrgyz Concept took Mike to the local Skoda garage. Skodas are made in Nizhny, not just for Russia but for quite a lot of the world. The town was the centre of Russian arms production during the Second World War and has a strong manufacturing history, so much so that foreigners were only allowed to visit the town in 1990.

The head of the Skoda dealership in the town was clearly quite a local personality. He assembled his whole team, who worked from 5 p.m. to 1.30 a.m. They entertained Mike, probably to keep him out of the mechanics' hair. Because Mike has worked in many different places around the world he has a great skill in getting on with people even when they share little in language. His rapport is particularly strong with technical people, who seem to sense in him a kindred spirit. At any rate the Skoda workers did a brilliant job on the brakes and when Mike offered to pay they not only refused point blank to accept any money but also showered him with gifts. I have since bought a Skoda Yeti car, one of the models made in Nizhny, partly influenced by the kindness of our friends there who helped us so generously.

The two teams of tour agents that looked after all of us on the rally also did a really good job. Both Nomads and Kyrgyz Concept really knew what they were doing in handling the myriad demands that come with the job of getting the rally drivers through unknown territory in China, Mongolia, Kazakhstan and Russia and made sure that all problems were handled. And an amazing proportion of these problems were handled very quickly as well. It would be invidious to single out individuals but for anyone visiting these countries, you couldn't hope for more able and committed people to look after your needs.

One of the features of this rally was that there were no widespread outbreaks of food poisoning or upset stomachs as had occurred on all previous Beijing to Paris rallies that my friends had described to me. As you can imagine, an outbreak of the local version of Montezuma's revenge in a camp of around 250 people with only five latrines can be somewhat unpleasant. Preparing food in camps in the desert cannot be an easy task and the fact that this was done efficiently and safely on each occasion made the rally a lot more comfortable than it might have been for us ralliers and apparently much more enjoyable than for its predecessors!

The car was purchased by Bentley guru Jeremy Padgett and he and his team, with Neville Garrad, 'Nev', in the lead, prepared it for the rally. That the car completed the rally and drove really well is a tribute to their work as well as to the underlying strength of the car. As Paul Guinness, editor of *Rolls-Royce and Bentley Driver*, put it in his article about the car, 'although traversing Lincolnshire's countryside over a single afternoon could hardly be compared with the full Peking to Paris experience, it certainly reinforced just what a highly capable – and competitive – machine this particular S1 has become'.[1]

Before we got started various people helped us particularly. John Butterworth put us in touch with a friend who owned the Land Rover testing facility. Although in the end we did not have the time to take advantage of the offer, it was a kind thought and much appreciated.

Giles Keating, who has been a close friend since he joined me in a two-person economic forecasting unit at the Confederation of British Industry (CBI) in the mid-1970s, gave us full use of his cottage and his forest in Snowdonia to test the car. We put about 300 miles on it driving back and forth and discovered some problems. All of this was done amongst some beautiful scenery looking out towards the coast. It was a great place to be and the testing gave us some very useful information about what worked and what didn't.

Various people who had entered the Peking Paris rally before were extremely generous with advice. My old classmate from when I was about eight years old in Malaysia, Rikkee Curtis (now Dato' Richard Curtis), had an excellent and lively supper with me. Sir Gerry Acher, who has completed the rally twice, gave up a morning to brief me at his club and gave me excellent advice. Mark Seligman, who sits on the Rector's Council with me at our old college, Lincoln College Oxford, also spent a couple of hours on the phone telling me what to do and what not to do. My good friend Martin Gilbert, co-founder of Aberdeen Asset Management and yet another with whom I had been at school in Malaysia, introduced me to his colleague Andrew Laing, an experienced rallier who had participated in the 2016 rally; his information over a glass or two of wine one evening proved invaluable.

Mum and Dad offered a decent sum of financial sponsorship which we greatly appreciated. It helped offset some of our costs. Dad also got up and made a very generous speech at our lunch in Paris the day after we arrived which was kind of him. He and Mum, both in their nineties, stood in blazing sunshine for a couple of hours in the Place Vendôme as we coped with the slightly chaotic arrival plans which the rally organisers had put in place.

Other sponsors included Sin Chai of Inverlochy Castle, a special friend and an amazing man who runs one of the top hotel chains in Europe, and Nick Browne of Nicholson Gin. And we also carried stickers for Fair Fuel, a wonderful campaign to keep down the cost of motoring, run by the indefatigable Howard Cox and Quentin Willson, and for Stellar Fuel Additives, run by my very good friend Kevin Mahoney.

On the rally we raised some money for the Harinder Veriah Trust. The late Harinder Veriah was married to Martin Jacques (former editor of the *Independent* and author of *When China Rules the World*) and sadly died very young in Hong Kong.* She had been educated at the Assunta Convent in Petaling Jaya, Malaysia, where my family have close connections.† The Trust raises money for poor girls at that school. Since my first bob-a-job week (when I was aged six) was for the same school it seems appropriate still to be trying to collect funds for them more than sixty years on. If any of the readers wish to support this excellent charity, where the funds raised actually go to the intended recipients and not to fundraisers or to administrators, please contact me through Cebr.

---

* Oddly, Harinder's late father, Karam Singh, had been one of my father's sparring partners when he was developing Petaling Jaya, Malaysia's first new town.

† My mother set up their kindergarten; my father chaired the fundraising committee to raise funds for their hospital. My mother even acted as Mother Superior when the actual Mother Superior was on holiday!

In getting this book finished in time, I have been helped by a number of people. First, my agent Martin Redfern of Northbank Talent Management recommended his former HarperCollins colleagues at whitefox. Chris Wold and Julia Koppitz from whitefox have done wonders in getting the book edited in time. And Miranda Ward has had the tough task of copyediting and has hugely improved my original draft.

The pictures in this book are from a variety of sources. I am grateful to Michael McWilliams, Lesley Garside and Liz Tanner for permission to include pictures which they took at various points on the rally.

But of course the greatest pressure from doing a rally like this is felt by one's family, from whom one is distracted by the preparation. Both Mike's wife, Rowena, and mine, Ianthe, were affected by this.

Ianthe in addition organised our Mongolian visas and had the huge success of organising a wonderful party in Paris for the day after we arrived. She worked tirelessly on this, dealing with the varying requirements of our friends. We are really proud that so many kindly turned up to meet us in Paris. We were grateful as well to Mike's son Chris and his partner Tamsin for not only turning up in Paris but particularly for looking after my parents in the Place Vendôme when the sun threatened to overcome them.

Of course the real hero of the rally was Mike. Before the rally he spent months building in compartments and storage in the Bentley. In addition, he arranged all the logistics for the trip. Once we got going, he did a lot of the driving, but more importantly he kept the car on the road. He worked appalling hours on the car and put himself under immense stress. Unfortunately I was not much help to him here, for which I apologise. Without him we certainly would not have made Paris.

So it is to Mike and to our families that I dedicate this book. Thanks so much for everything.

Douglas McWilliams
Tenterden
December 2019

PROLOGUE

Have you ever imagined what it might be like to take a fairly standard luxury saloon, designed to take ministers and tycoons about their business, across the Gobi Desert on camel tracks in the world's hardest endurance rally from Beijing to Paris?

Or what it is like to drive the whole distance of the old Silk Road, soon to be revitalised via China's Belt and Road Initiative, which connects China with the West by land?

Or what the coming together of the revitalised Russia and China means for the West?

My brother Mike and I decided after a lively family Christmas dinner in 2016 to enter a Bentley S1 in the Peking to Paris endurance rally.

We had to find the car, work out how to afford the rally, set up the car for the rally and ship it to Beijing. Preparations for the rally included receiving nineteen injections from the world's foremost travel doctor (whose next appointment was to cancel the Rolling Stones' US tour on medical grounds), arranging multiple insurances, and getting three visas – each of which would take a week to process – in the one-month window when they could be issued and still valid.

How did we do it, and what happened to us on the rally? Who did we meet and what did we see? What is an economist's take on driving all the way across China, Russia and Mongolia as well as emerging Eastern Europe, Germany, Belgium and France? What is an energy expert's perspective on driving across one of the world's great oil producers and through some of the largest wind and solar farms in the world?

This book is about a drive across the entire Eurasian continent in a Bentley S1 in the world's greatest endurance rally. Our story would be an interesting one even if this were 'just' a travel book about a rather exotic trip on an adventurous rally. But we entered the rally because we sensed that the world's centre of economic gravity was changing and moving towards the area that we were traversing: China, Central Asia and Russia. We wanted to see this happening at first hand.

I have the good fortune to have founded and still to play a part in running the London-based international economic consultancy, the Centre for Economics and Business Research (Cebr). As an observer of the world economy and author of reports on the Chinese Belt and Road Initiative, I wanted to see the world's shifting economic tectonic plates for myself.

For the past 500 years the world has seemed, at least to Western eyes, to have been centred on Western Europe and the Western European offshoots, mainly in North America. During the first three quarters of the twentieth century these made up more than 50 per cent of world GDP in most conventional estimates.* Since 1975 this share has fallen back to around 30 per cent as other economies in Asia, Latin America and Central and Eastern Europe have grown, often at astonishingly rapid rates. The last time the share of the Western economies was as low as this was in the early part of the nineteenth century, before economic development in North America spread west.

From the time of Marco Polo there has been a fascination with the land route from Western Europe and the Middle East to China. But the Ottomans closed off this route in the fifteenth century and a plausible explanation for the century of naval exploration that followed in the late fifteenth and early sixteenth centuries was that the Western European economies were looking to find an alternative route to retain access to the exotic products, like silks and spices, that had previously flowed down the Silk Road.

From the fifteenth to the nineteenth centuries, the land routes from Asia to Europe declined in importance as the new sea routes around the world replaced them. But towards the end of the nineteenth and in the early part of the twentieth century a new generation of explorers revisited these routes. Indeed the phrase 'The Silk Road' was invented by the German explorer Baron von Richthofen in 1877.[2] Then the emergence of the Soviet Union made exploration difficult,

---

* Most of us economists use the Groningen University Growth and Development Centre data for this type of comparison: www.rug.nl/ggdc/ historicaldevelopment/maddison. Also useful is https://ourworldindata.org/ from the wonderful Max Roser at Oxford University.

and this difficulty was enhanced when China also became Communist and also imposed strict controls on travel, let alone exploration.

For fifty years the land route from Asia to Europe was effectively blocked. But underneath the surface economic pressures were building up that eventually led to its reopening.

East Asia's importance in world Gross Domestic Product (GDP) has been rising dramatically with so-called globalisation. In 1968, when the first offshore factories appeared in Hong Kong, the East Asian share of world GDP was only 3 per cent. Today it is 25 per cent, catching up with the whole of the Western economies. It would be reasonable to expect that East Asia will be of similar economic size to the Western economies at some point in the 2020s or 2030s.

Currently Russia, the former Soviet Union republics plus Mongolia comprise about 4 per cent of world GDP. But one of the key arguments of this book is that this is about to change. The Belt and Road Initiative links China, Central Asia, Russia and Western Europe. As a result Russia and Central Asia will move from being in many ways part of the world's economic periphery towards the centre. The scope for minerals exploitation in the area is huge and has been constrained so far by the lack of transport infrastructure. As the Cebr study on the Belt and Road Initiative shows, this is changing as the initiative delivers this infrastructure. Using conventional economic analysis, the study shows that the initiative should boost GDP in Mongolia by the huge amount of more than a third.* And obviously the potential is for much more economic activity to be unlocked as exploitation of minerals becomes much more financially viable as a result of transport infrastructure.

Driving the Silk Road is about driving through these changing economic landscapes, across China, covering the Gobi Desert in Mongolia, then through Siberia, Kazakhstan, the rest of Russia and into Western Europe, ending in the Place Vendôme in Paris. In particular, it's about what this looked like to me, as an economist, and to my brother, as an energy engineer. We both concluded that the rest of the world ignores the changes in China, Russia and Central Asia at its peril. The geographical centre of the world is starting to become the world's economic hub.

But the book also tells of the huge distances involved, what it is like to travel by car (admittedly a very luxurious car) across half the world, of the conflict within the rally between those who were serious ralliers and those who simply wanted to reach the finish, and of the wonderful people we met on the way and the scenery that we were able to see. And, of course, of how two brothers who had not spent so much time together since we were children managed to survive thirty-six days of close proximity.

---

* If an economic study indicates an impact as great as a third, the likelihood is that the real impact will be very large and could be anything between a bit less than a third and as much as a doubling of GDP.

The good news is that we got there. Though we must have had a guardian angel looking over us – for example when we holed our petrol tank a few hundred metres away from the only petrol station for 150 kilometres.

Still, we were one of only 21 cars out of 106 to complete the rally without being flatbedded or towed. We didn't quite travel halfway round the world – the circumference of the world at 44 degrees latitude (halfway between Beijing at 39 degrees and Paris at 48 degrees) is 39,990 kilometres. We travelled about 16,000 kilometres in total (after allowing for navigational mistakes) which is 40 per cent of the whole way round the world at that latitude. So we were not far short of halfway round the world. Our remarkable Bentley did us proud to take us so far and allow us to visit so many places.

1

INTRODUCTION

Near the end of a splendid Christmas dinner in 2016 I suggested to my brother Mike that it might be fun to enter the Peking to Paris Motor Challenge. It must have been a good dinner: Mike, who is normally the sensible one, agreed.

Our father had driven S-series Bentleys when we were young, and from that I'd discovered how fundamentally strong they were. This suggested an intriguing possibility – why not undertake the rally in a car normally used to chauffeur ministers and tycoons?

From the internet I learned of the famous Bentley guru Jeremy Padgett and phoned him up to discuss my mad idea. Jeremy confirmed it was feasible, and that an S1 would be best.

So we sent in our entry forms and started trying to find a car. Jeremy was very helpful and went to inspect what he called the 'donor car' in Essex. He said it was suitable and I bought it unseen. It had a particular advantage: in the 1970s all four wings had been replaced with fibreglass items for £751, and this proved to be really useful on the rally.*

---

* Technically non-standard fibreglass wings are not permitted under the rally regulations. However the rally organisers are reasonably sensible about compliance. I wrote to them some months in advance explaining the situation and also that the non-standard wings had been fitted nearly fifty years ago (backed up by the appropriate invoices). They agreed that since we were clearly not trying to gain an inappropriate advantage an exemption could be permitted in our case.

Details of Jeremy's work are described in *Rolls-Royce and Bentley Driver* Issue 11, so I won't repeat them here. Suffice to say we were able to use some upgrades that were available when the car was made in the 1950s. At that time Bentley offered what they called 'colonial spec', which included stronger suspension for use in the bush in Africa, or for wealthy Australian farmers who had done well out of the Korean War commodities boom in the early 1950s and who were cashing in with a fancy car. Other than that the car was lightly modified, with a better air filter, slightly raised suspension (not nearly enough, as it transpired) and off-road tyres.

A good friend, Giles Keating, has a forest in Snowdonia where he let us test the car on the gravel tracks. After about 300 miles of aggressive shaking down, we were amazed by the off-road handling. We took it back to Padgett's for the final modifications. With the fixes completed Mike took the car and fitted it out, attaching straps, containers to replace the rear seat and a wide range of tools and spares for the rally.

The car was collected in mid-March, and shipped to Beijing. We were excited to be reunited with it a couple of days before the rally, to make the final preparations.

After briefings from the Chief of Traffic Police on driving in China and from the rally organisers, a last-minute shopping expedition for supplies, a splendid sending-off dinner, scrutineering and an afternoon applying sponsors' stickers we were woken at 5 a.m. to leave for the Great Wall for the official start.

We had colourful and noisy celebrations with lion dancers, stilt walkers and drummers, and then we set off.

The first day's driving was a gentle introduction to China, enabling us to be amazed at the scale of the infrastructural development. We ended in the fastest-growing large city in the world, Hohhot, capital of Inner Mongolia. It used to be China's dairy capital but is now a centre for big data. It has a population of 3 million, up from 1 million a decade ago. I counted sixty-one cranes. Naturally the traffic jams were on an epic scale!

After another day of fairly gentle driving and a border crossing that lasted for most of the day, we were excited to enter the Gobi Desert in Mongolia.

This is the heart of the rally and the section that determines one's overall performance on the event. Our aim was simply to get to the end under our own steam so we weren't particularly worried about our place in the rally classification. Those who had been on previous rallies said that this year's was the most difficult by far for two different reasons – the route covered much tougher and more undulating terrain and the distances which we were expected to achieve in a day were more demanding, meaning that we had to drive far faster. The toughness was particularly severe for those of us at the back of the field starting late since our objective of arriving before nightfall was rarely achieved in the desert and once it got dark everything got about ten times more difficult.

But we would never have missed it – the sheer beauty of the countryside was spectacular and this was a unique opportunity to go far off the beaten track.

Driving across the desert was gruelling, particularly for those of us with larger-engined cars that were forced to start late on in the day. We missed the advantage of being able to get going when it was cool and almost inevitably ended up having to drive in the dark. Everyone had told us we shouldn't do this, but if we were to collect crucial supplies of petrol and food in camp there seemed no other way. The pace was relentless and eventually three problems emerged that were to haunt us for the rest of the rally.

We holed the lower fuel tank; the braking system gave way (not only the mechanical system but also the two servo systems); and the suspension and steering got badly damaged. Fortunately we had installed an additional fuel tank in the boot and were able to spatchcock a fix from the upper fuel tank. But this meant that we could take only 70 litres of fuel, severely limiting our range. We were really grateful to Alan and Steve Maden, rallying a Silver Shadow from the 1970s, who lent us two 20-litre bladders, enabling us to finish.

The brakes were a persistent problem: after China we had no low-speed braking, and the servo-driven hydraulic system was poor at best and, at times, non-existent. And on one occasion the brakes seized on and we could only progress by disconnecting that particular system. After the engine stalled on a long hill climb, we had to reverse into a bank to avoid rolling back 500 metres downhill. The fibreglass wings came into their own, cushioning the impact. Later that day we drove the last 50 kilometres to camp in the dark with no brakes at all.

Despite all the problems the car was solid and drove beautifully. Handling, both on the dirt and on tar, was exceptional for a car of this size, and we luxuriated in the leather armchairs, having retained the original front seats. These really came into their own on the night we had to sleep in the car.

We made it through Mongolia, just. During the rest day in Ulaanbaatar Mike did his best with the brakes and later on found some cracks in the rear chassis. He took it to a local welder who found a scrap piece of angle iron in his backyard and welded it on to the chassis. It is now a permanent fixture. By the time we got to Novosibirsk the driver's side front wheel was hanging at an unusual angle. Again the local bush mechanics came to our rescue. The driver's side cross pin had sheared in two places, leaving the steering arms dangling. They took the broken part to a local metal worker who turned and threaded a replica part from scratch.

After the Gobi Desert we still had two-thirds of the rally to go and problems stemming from the breakages in the desert continued to haunt us. But at least the most difficult driving was over.

We missed the ambassador's wife, a friend, who had come to our hotel to welcome us in Nur-Sultan (formerly Astana) in Kazakhstan because the replacement for our failed fuel pump was fitted the wrong way round. In Nizhny Novgorod the brakes were squealing to such an extent that we had to take the car to the local Skoda garage to put on replacement shoes. Their team worked from 5 p.m. till 1.30 a.m. to fix the problem and when Mike asked to pay, they not only refused it but – as mentioned in the foreword – showered him with gifts, of which the most impressive were a Russian army cape from World War 2 and an entrenching tool captured from the Germans in the same war.

In all the car came to a halt on fourteen of the thirty-six days of the rally. But Mike's mechanical skills and those of the rally mechanics, the so-called 'sweeps', meant that we were able to get going again.

And we made it to the finish. Allegedly only twenty-one cars completed the rally under their own steam without being flatbedded or towed, though there is no comprehensive record. We were possibly the most standard of all the cars to do so. It was a joyous sight to arrive at the finishing line on the Place Vendôme in Paris and discover our parents, who had stood for two hours in blazing sun waiting for us, with our wives, family and so many friends. We had achieved what we set out to do, which was to prove that a largely standard Bentley S1 could complete the Peking to Paris rally under its own steam. Well done to those who made the car over sixty years ago!

2

GETTING STARTED

My brother Mike and I were brought up in the Far East, in Malaysia. Mike was actually born there; I was aged one when our parents emigrated from Longridge in Lancashire to Malacca in 1953.

We both grew up in the face of an enormous chasm between the East and the West. The first two times I travelled from Britain to Malaya, as it was then called, I travelled by ship, taking roughly six weeks each time. Western newspapers, printed on tissue-thin paper to travel by airmail, arrived about a week late until the 1980s.

There were occasional tales of intrepid adventurers who had driven 'home' from Malaysia. These were often planters on rubber estates, used to living with few other Westerners nearby, hardy and self-reliant people, often Scots (and indeed often Aberdonians, like Martin Gilbert's father Jimmy). Driving from Asia to Europe seemed wildly exciting. From memory the only man I met who had actually done this did so in an MG sports car, an improbable vehicle for such a trek. But copying them in driving from East to West became an ambition for an impressionable child.

I've been fairly lucky in my career as an economist, achieving high-profile posts like becoming the Chief Economic Adviser to the Confederation of British Industry and Chief Economist for IBM UK before eventually founding and running the well-known economic consultancy Cebr. What success my colleagues and I have had was heavily based on the understanding of the impact of globalisation remembered from my youth (which was the basis of my MPhil thesis at Oxford in 1974) and (post the stint at IBM) combining that with an understanding of the economic impact of technology.

I also had the good fortune to be chosen from over 300 applicants to be the Gresham Professor of Commerce in 2011 and my lectures focused on what I called the world's greatest ever economic event, the impact of China's economic development on the rest of the world. For most of my life it has seemed obvious that this would be transformative and one of my enduring frustrations has been the failure of so many other economists to understand this, especially those economists who work in government, academia and journalism.

My thesis at Oxford was an analysis of the economic impact of the first two offshore electronic plants near Kuala Lumpur. The gains for all sides were huge. Both investments were entirely paid off in a year. I told my professors at Oxford that this was going to be the future. They told me I was talking nonsense... I have had a degree of scepticism about economics professors ever since.

Having lectured and written about how economic development in the East is changing the world, I really wanted to experience the land route from Asia to Europe for myself. The Chinese government had announced the Belt and Road Initiative (BRI), developing infrastructure linking China to Europe. And books with 'Silk Road' in their title were starting to appear, suggesting a growing interest in this link as the rising volume of trade between East and West was beginning to make the connecting infrastructure between Asia and Europe economically viable.

Cars have been part of my life since I was a child. My parents claim that I largely taught myself to read when I was three years old using old copies of *Autocar* and *Motor*. They had left me with a family friend in Malacca, the manager of Wearne Brothers, the local agents for Ford, while they went to visit what would eventually prove to be the site of my father's next job developing the new town of Petaling Jaya. I had apparently settled down in a corner and spent the entire day happily devouring about a hundred back issues of the magazines. The upside was that by the end I could read pretty well for a three-year-old. The downside was a somewhat restricted vocabulary with a marked bias towards mechanical words and phrases. Certainly I learned the meaning of SU carburettors, MacPherson struts and De Dion rear axles at an early stage.

From then on cars fascinated me. Whenever I saw a car that I had never seen before I would pressurise my parents to stop so that I could have a look at it. My father's memoirs claim that at the age of four or five I suddenly shouted 'Look Dad, a Bristol' and made him stop his car so that I could look more closely at what I had correctly observed to be a Bristol despite recognising it only from pictures. I collected Dinky cars and made my long-suffering parents take me to motor shows and motor races, of which my favourite was the 1961 Easter Monday meeting at Goodwood where I was able to watch my hero Stirling Moss.

My car ownership history has generally been a triumph of hope over common sense. I have had a long history of running cars the upkeep of which I could not afford and of break-downs resulting from underinvestment in maintenance. Only in recent months, in my sixty-eighth year, have I for the very first time ever bought a sensible car, a Skoda Yeti, chosen for its ability to go down a steep drive without grounding and fit (with inches to spare) round a tight bend into my garage as well as in homage to the wonderful mechanics at the Skoda dealership in Nizhny Novgorod who helped us on the rally.

Even my romantic life was determined by cars – I met my wife Ianthe when my Triumph TR6 sports car broke down on my way to another wedding and she kindly gave me a lift. When I possessed a classic Aston Martin DB6 Mark II, Ianthe and I managed two exciting drives: the route of the 1955 Mille Miglia sports car race in Italy (Stirling Moss won the original race in ten hours and seven minutes; we, travelling at a more leisurely pace, took ten days); and a 7,000-mile drive all around the United States culminating in the really fancy Pebble Beach classic car show.

On this latter drive I gave several talks, but the most interesting was when I was a speaker at the dinner of the Aston Martin Owners Club in the Monterey Aquarium on Steinbeck's Cannery Row. The other two attractions at the dinner were the diver from the shark tank (only a rumour that his nickname was 'Stumpy') speaking from the tank itself, surrounded by sharks, and the widow of the Le Mans winner and car legend Carroll Shelby. In fact they had a choice of widows, since he had been married eight times! Since the one they chose made a slightly disjointed and rather disreputable speech and was finally led away swaying, they probably would have done better to choose one of the other seven. In any event it was left to me to try to put the evening back on an even keel. I hope I succeeded.

When Mike and I were young, our dad always had interesting cars. When the *Daily Telegraph* one weekend published a list of the hundred most beautiful cars ever made, Dad, Mum, Mike and I calculated that at one time or other we had between us owned nearly twenty of them. At the age of eight I was taken to the Jaguar factory with my mother to collect a brand new Mark II Jaguar. Six years later my parents picked up a new W108 250SE Mercedes from the factory in Stuttgart. Two years later my father swopped the Mercedes for a Bentley S2.

As a family we loved the Bentley. As a teenager I occasionally tried it out (without permission) when the parents weren't around. Sadly when my mother tried the same thing she bashed it on the gatepost and had to phone my father, who was abroad, to break the bad news. He took it rather better than I suspect most husbands would have...

So in 2016, at the end of a splendid Christmas lunch cooked by our wonderful wives Ianthe and Rowena, I suggested to Mike that I had always wanted to drive the Paris Peking endurance rally in an S-series Bentley and asked if he would be interested in participating with me the next time the rally was due to be held, in 2019. I was delighted when he said yes. Mike is not only my brother but a distinguished engineer. He has built many dams. But he has an instinctive affinity with cars and anything else mechanical. I cannot think of anyone with whom I would rather go into the desert.

Some of our friends and acquaintances had driven this rally before. Rikkee Curtis, who had been in my class at school in Malaysia, had twice driven the rally with His Royal Highness the Sultan of Selangor (to whom my father is the Dato' Sri Selera, a sort of knight of the round table whose title means official food taster!). I had once when I was young spent an afternoon cooking satay with the man who is now Sultan (he was then called the Raja Muda, the crown prince) at a party given at his father's house in Sunningdale (bought from Diana Dors, with a prominent mirror on the ceiling above the bed!). Mark Seligman, a city grandee who sits with me on the Rector's Council of our old Oxford college, has completed the rally once. Sir Gerald Acher, the former head of accountants KPMG and another grandee whom I have met as economic adviser to both the CBI and the ICAEW (Institute of Chartered Accountants in England and Wales), had also completed the rally twice. And I was introduced to Andrew Laing, a colleague at Aberdeen Standard working with yet another old school friend from Malaysia, Martin Gilbert. Andrew participated in Peking Paris in 2016 and his tips were highly useful.

Mike and I both thought that a Bentley like Dad's old one would be excellent. They were strong cars and the first requirement for any car on this rally was strength. The second requirement was comfort, and what could be more comfortable than a Bentley? After a bit of research we decided that the S1 would be better than the later models. The iron engine, dating back to the 1920s, was famously robust and had powered many military vehicles in deserts and elsewhere and so was likely also to be strong enough for crossing the Gobi Desert. The S1 was the last vehicle powered by this engine, which had originally been designed for the Rolls-Royce Twenty series, launched in 1922.

The downside of the Bentley is its size and the length of its overhangs. The back of the car was grounded on many occasions while we crossed gullies in the Gobi Desert and finished the rally looking pretty fully depreciated.

To turn the car into an endurance rally weapon Padgett's team gave it a complete mechanical stripdown, only leaving the exterior and interior trim untouched. Suspension was renewed and upgraded to 'colonial specification', the tougher specification that Bentley used to make available in the 1950s for senior officials and businessmen in the former colonies with unpaved roads. The engine was uprated to Jeremy Padgett's standard specification, upgrading both BHP and torque. The gearbox was replaced with a unit from Graham Whitehouse. Interestingly I've had a unit from the same source before – my Aston Martin DB6 was also upgraded using a Graham Whitehouse automatic gearbox. In the Aston the upgrade allegedly reduced the power loss from 17 per cent to 4 per cent.

We probably didn't need to do much to the engine. But Jeremy Padgett's party trick is a series of upgrades that boost both power and torque from this engine by nearly 50 per cent each and it seemed a false economy to take the car to him and not take advantage of this option. His modifications included forged alloy pistons, electronic ignition, a bespoke stainless steel exhaust system and a lightweight alloy radiator as well as a pair of two-inch SU HD8 carburettors. The air filter was replaced with a trio of specially modified K&N filters which are not only effective but can also be washed out and reoiled. The modifications were developed by Jeremy Padgett and his father Alan together with the late Christian Hueber II, doyen of Bentley Continental owners and author of the definitive book about that model. The use of these modifications in Mr Hueber's Bentley is described in an article on the Saltwood Castle website[3] and is also described at greater length in an article in the late Alan Clark's book *Backfire*.[4] Both articles conclude that with the uprated engine Mr Hueber's car was in Clark's words 'extremely fast, with a remarkable increase in power'.

We left the exterior and the interior largely unmolested. The rally would sandblast the outsides so there wasn't much point smartening it up, while the inside was already comfortable and nicely patinated and quite likely to get soaked when driving through rivers.

Where we made changes was to fit the equipment needed for the rally. The exhaust was rerouted to the side with a 'snorkel' that could be attached, taking it up to waist height when driving through water. The ride height was raised nearly two inches at the front. An additional 100-litre extended range fuel tank was built, though we were never quite able to fill it up because the maximum credit limit permitted per transaction was normally reached before the tank was full!

The standard Avon tyres were replaced by Falken Wildpeak off-road tyres. Allegedly they are guaranteed for 50,000 miles though we never tested to see if the guarantee would hold in the Gobi Desert. As we only took three spares with us, one of the tyres made it through the whole rally unchanged and is still on the car.

Under the car was built a set of bolt-on aluminium panels running most of the length of the car to protect the underneath from damage from rocks and debris. While the panels might have helped in some cases, not only did they not help when the petrol tank got holed, but they led to a build-up of solidified mud between the panels and the floor of the car which was one of the reasons why we had problems with fuel lines and brakes on the rally.

To make the rally trip comfortable we also fitted air conditioning and a fridge. Some of our German rally colleagues joked that we had our own 'minibar' but the truth was more prosaic – the fridge kept our drinking water cool. However, post rally when the car has been exhibited at car shows it provides an entertaining sight as we use it as a base to dispense gin and tonic.

On the road the car has been a revelation. It drives more like a sports saloon than a staid limousine. Acceleration is sprightly while the suspension modifications mean that the car seems much more planted on the surface than a standard S1. The removal of the rear silencer means that progress can be heard but it is never raucous.

LEARNING ABOUT RALLYING

I booked Mike and myself on a one-day rally navigating course to be followed by a day's rallying from a golf course in Buckinghamshire. This proved brilliant and was money well spent. We learned about tulip maps and rally phrases such as 'rally time', which is the convention that for rallying purposes, if a rally crosses time zones, the 'rally time' is determined by the time zone in which the rally starts the day. (There was an interesting confusion with this on the actual rally in Kazakhstan near the Russian border, where the iPhone signal came across the border from Russia and our phones gave us a rally time one hour out.) The practice rally was great fun and we enjoyed trying to wind the car round tight courses. We didn't even come last and comfortably beat our main large car rival, a Mercedes driven by a friend whom I had met previously on an Aston Martin tour of Ireland.

TESTING IN WALES

In November 2018 Ianthe, Rowena, Mike and I spent a weekend in Wales at Giles Keating's cottage in Snowdonia, close to Blaenau Ffestiniog, the stop on the Ffestiniog Railway. I'd known Giles since we first worked together for the CBI in 1976 and we had always enjoyed each other's company. Oddly, when we first met, Giles' father was the most prominent building and civil engineering arbitrator in the UK, a profession that my father was about to join when he qualified as a barrister at the age of fifty after retiring from his activities in Malaysia as a civil engineer.* Giles' father and mine ended up in the two opposing leading chambers of barristers specialising in building cases, which was slightly odd when their sons were sharing an office and just occasionally meant that one of us had to shut his ears when the other was receiving a parental phone call.

Giles eventually joined Credit Suisse First Boston, initially as an economist, then as head of research and eventually as a private investment adviser. Like many in the city in the period post big bang he had to find outlets for tax-efficient investment and with the rise of China creating a demand for commodities, the tax breaks for investment in forestry proved especially attractive. Moreover, they encouraged the purchase of forests in wonderfully beautiful places such as Snowdonia. Giles' forest proved ideal for our testing – the tracks had been appropriately chewed up by timber lorries so that driving at speed was surprisingly similar to driving through the Gobi Desert. During the testing three problems emerged: the brakes got stuck, there seemed to be a problem with the carburettor linkage and a problem with the electrics appeared. Although Padgett's had a go at fixing these problems, they all reappeared on the rally.

---

* The Malays have a saying that a man aged fifty should change either his job or his wife. Fortunately my father did the former.

RALLY PREPARATION WEEKEND IN GAYDON

One of the features of the Peking Paris rally is the two-day briefing session which the organisers set up about eight months before the start of the rally to help you deal with some of the problems that can be handled in advance. This year the briefing session was held in the Museum of the British Motor Industry in Gaydon. The ralliers were briefed on key elements of the rally like the medical and insurance requirements, the visas we would need and the key elements of the route. Quite a few came (as we did) in their rally cars, but some used the opportunity as a chance to show off other cars in their collections. One Gulf-liveried Ford GT40 looked a highly improbable entrant with ground clearance of around two and a half inches.

The briefing was carried out very professionally, and we got the chance to test navigation equipment and meet other ralliers. We also collected our prize possessions – the specially designed rally jackets only available to those on the rally. We made a few good friends at the Gaydon briefing session, particularly John Young, with whom we had a curry in the evening in the middle of the two-day session. John proved a gold mine of useful information. His phrase that when the ralliers get into Mongolia a 'red mist' seems to descend on them has stuck in our minds and led to a brilliant painting by Mike's wife Rowena. Apparently when many of the ralliers get on to the open roads in the desert they rush off like dogs let off a leash. Both at the time when he told us this and on the rally we were surprised by the idea but it was undoubtedly true and there were a number of accidents on the first two days caused by this excess of excitement.

MIKE'S FITTING OUT

After Gaydon and the testing in Giles' forest, we sent the car back to Padgett's for final fettling. Then we picked it up. I took the car with me when invited to a Foreign Office briefing for the so-called 'great and good' (not sure how I qualified!) on Russia at the Foreign Office conference centre at Wilton Park and quite remarkably the car was reunited with someone who had travelled in it more than fifty years previously. Roger Munnings, chairman of the Russo-British Chamber of Commerce, a fixture on the Moscow scene for many years and an independent director of Lukoil, was co-chairing the briefing and had once travelled in the selfsame car in the late 1960s when visiting a girlfriend's parents. Obviously the car was prominent in the car park at Wilton Park with its rally plates and its distinctive registration number (RFW 100) and during the conference he suddenly approached me and kindly gave me a note explaining his connection with it. The car attracted a lot of attention with the Russians, particularly when I promised that I would drive it all the way across Russia.

I had rather casually thought that once Padgett's had finished with the car it was roughly ready to go. But I hadn't really got to grips with Mike's planning and engineering approach. He then took the car, built wooden compartments for the back where the seat had been removed, and strapped in tyres, tools and spares, removing window winders and ashtrays. He was immensely thorough. He also built in a compartment in the front of the car between the seats which has proved so useful that it has been kept since the car was sent to be refurbished.

He must have spent many hours putting this together, getting all the spares and equipment we needed and buying tools. He was very proud on the rally to discover he had quite a number of tools that the rally mechanics, the sweeps, did not have. The car was superbly equipped and this was one of the key factors that enabled us to survive the rally, since we had replacements for virtually everything that broke.

In addition to car equipment, one of the requirements for the rally was that we be equipped for six nights camping. This was a horror to which I intended to steel myself, but I had no expectation of liking it. Mike was very kind and constructed a huge tent (which proved surprisingly easy to set up, even in the dark) with separate sleeping compartments and a middle area. One of the Italians claimed that this was 'not a tent – it's an apartment'. Mike even provided me with an extra pillow (a real one, not one of those metaphorical ones that often turn up uninvited in cheaper hotels). We were truly living as close to the lap of luxury as one could when camping. Though I still hope never to have to camp again! Mike also told me what to pack and allowed a couple of shirts and a couple of pairs of trousers. Fortunately they proved quick drying, though occasionally the final drying was driven by my body warmth.

Thus equipped, the car was picked up by Cars UK and delivered to their depot near Norwich. We would next see it in Beijing.

MEDICAL

Once we had sorted out the car, attention turned to ourselves and our bodies. Mike's doctor is his Monday evening tennis partner, Dr David Dodds (who is now my doctor too). Mike is a regular traveller to 'interesting' parts of the world and is already fairly well inoculated. But David put together a first aid kit for him that proved useful on the rally.

I was advised by Gerry Acher to visit Dr Richard Dawood, who is the guru of travel medicine. Richard looked through the map of where I was going and announced I would need nineteen injections. I often think that physical courage is over-rated and moral courage underrated, and I felt that on this occasion I showed rather too much physical courage and too little moral courage in failing to dispute this. No one else on the rally seemed to require quite so many vaccinations.

Anyway I had the vaccinations, including three anti-rabies (rather less severe than when I was younger, when anti-rabies injections had to be applied through the wall of the stomach) over three visits. Interestingly it turned out that Richard's next appointment was with Rolling Stone Mick Jagger in Florida. It was only when I read the newspapers a couple of days later that I discovered that this was rather more than a routine visit, since the Stones' US tour had been cancelled and Mick had ended up in hospital for a heart procedure.

Richard Dawood put together a serious first aid kit that looked likely to cover a wide range of potential emergencies, not just for us two but in case we came upon an emergency affecting someone else on the rally. Unfortunately by the time we had packed everything this turned out to be hard to locate and when I picked up strep throat on the rally Mike's medical pack turned out to be the one I used for antibiotics.

VISAS

As soon as the rally excitement builds up you start to want to get your visas. But it doesn't work that way. You can't book a visa until a month before you travel, since otherwise it will have expired before you can use it.

For the rally we needed three visas, for China, for Mongolia and for Russia. For each we had to fill in a form online through a system that kept crashing and required immense quantities of detail. Each country charged a rip-off fee that might have deterred more casual visitors. Each claimed to require your passport for a week but in fact would return it slightly quicker if you paid yet another additional fee. In addition the Russian passport office (fortunately close to my office) managed to find national holidays justifying its closure on about eight of the twelve days open to us to get the visas. In the end we got the visas after a lot of angst, but only managed to have them all fully completed five days before we were due to fly out. I was only able to hand Mike's passport back to him when we met at Heathrow to fly to Beijing.

BELT AND ROAD REPORT

As if we hadn't made our lives complicated enough, I had also created yet another rod for my own back. As part of the financing of our participation in the rally, Cebr had negotiated sponsorship of a report on the area over which we were about to rally, to cover the economic impact of the Chinese Belt and Road Initiative.

The only problem was that this report had to be written. Sponsorship was confirmed with only about three weeks left to perform the analysis and write the report. Pablo Shah especially, with some help from Kay Neufeld in the office and from Mike, helped me a lot but I still had to write nearly 15,000 words in about a week.

Graham Robinson had brilliantly obtained sponsorship from the Chartered Institute of Building and we managed to finalise the report and print off copies and press releases in the final three days before we left for China. We released the report in Beijing on the Monday before the rally. It was well received in both the Chinese and international press, but it meant that the week before travelling passed in a blur. Some of the report is included in this book, since it describes the infra-structure that is being created and its effect on the countries that we travelled across.

HEATHROW

After all the fun with the visas we were quite relieved when Ianthe, Rowena, Mike and I were able to meet at Heathrow for our flight to Beijing and I could hand over Mike's passport to him. We seemed to have been racing pretty well continu-ously to complete everything necessary before we left, so it was quite a relief when we all arrived at the airport at roughly the same time with nothing else going wrong.

I don't really remember the flight. I must have been so relieved to have got on the plane with all the formalities completed that I suspect I must have fallen asleep pretty well immediately.

When I woke up we were arriving in Beijing airport. One of the slightly scary highlights here is a screen which when you pass shows not only your face, but also your name and your flight – and if you are on a departing flight, whether you are late or not. I had heard about this but somehow had not quite expected the technology to work effectively. But it does. Welcome to China, land of facial recognition!

3

THE SILK ROADS

THE SILK ROOM

The rally connects Asia with Europe and (very approximately) follows the routes of the historic Silk Roads. So it is interesting to see how these routes have developed over time.

From ancient history onwards there have been trails connecting Europe with Central Asia and the Far East. The consensus seems to be that they started to emerge during the second century BCE. Allegedly the trails developed because Chinese soils lacked selenium, a deficiency that led to frailness and reduced growth in horses to such an extent that they could not support an armoured rider. The Chinese wanted to buy the much stronger horses from the steppes and were prepared to trade products, especially grain and silk, in exchange for them.

These trails connected not only with Central Asia but extended to Persia and the Persian Royal Road, India and eventually to the system of Roman roads that were being constructed across Europe and around the Mediterranean around the same time. To justify the costs of transportation and security (goods passing through the Silk Roads required protection which was provided at considerable expense to the travellers by local tribesmen) the goods transported tended to be luxury products.

The phrases 'Silk Road' and 'Silk Roads' tend today to be used interchangeably. But in fact there were a number of different roads traversing roughly the same route. These different roads emerged, mainly, it appears, to create competition to limit the escalating costs of protection and security on any individual road.

The western end of the Silk Roads were initially determined by economics. The markets that had sufficient spending power to justify the infrastructural expenditure that would pay for a Silk Road link can be worked out from the GDP data. According to the Maddison Project data held at the Groningen Growth and Development Centre at Groningen University, the world's largest economies in the year 1 CE were as given in Table 1. It can be seen that the Mediterranean markets were by far the largest in Europe. At the beginning of the first millennium, the whole of Northern Europe including Scandinavia, Germany, Benelux and the UK had a GDP roughly equivalent to that of France alone. So the southern end of the Silk Road ended in Persia, Turkey and Italy where it provided access to the larger markets in Southern Europe.

These routes were used for nearly a millennium and a half. The volume of trade was not high but enabled products, cultures and, especially, religions to spread between Europe, the Middle East and Asia.

But all this came to an end when the routes were closed in 1453 by the Ottoman Empire. The Mongol Empire started to

Table 1: World's Largest Economies in Year 1 CE (Data here from
Groningen University)

COUNTRY	GDP AT 1990 GEARY-KHAMIS DOLLARS ($ MILLIONS)	GDP PER CAPITA
INDIA	33,750	450
CHINA	26,820	450
ITALY	6,475	809
TURKEY	4,400	550
EGYPT	2,700	600
FRANCE	2,366	473
IRAN	2,000	500
SPAIN	1,867	498
NORTHERN EUROPE*	2,305	c.400

break up after the death of Kublai Khan in 1294. The routes
were kept functional by the Samarkand-based conqueror
Tamburlaine until his death in 1405, but after that warfare
and anarchy meant that in practical terms it was not a great
idea to use them for trade because the price of protection
exceeded the profits on the goods traded.

The closure of the Silk Roads led to the 'Age of Discovery',
as intrepid sailors from the maritime nations explored the
world by sea, seeking replacements for the land route. This
resulted in the emergence of sea routes around the world and,
of course, to the so-called 'discovery' of the Americas.

---

* Germany, Austria, Belgium, the Netherlands, Sweden, Norway, Denmark,
Finland, Switzerland and the UK.

In the West we tend to associate the Silk Roads with Marco Polo. But in fact the phrase Silk Road was coined more recently, by the German explorer Baron Ferdinand von Richthofen* who used the phrase *Seidenstrasse* (Silk Road) in 1877 in a three-volume book under the title of *China: Ergebnisse eigener Reisen und darauf gegründeter Studien.*

Much of what we currently know about the Silk Roads emerged from geographers and explorers who investigated in the late nineteenth and early twentieth centuries. And of course the first motor trip across the area was the first Peking to Paris race in 1907, well chronicled in Luigi Barzini's book *Peking to Paris: A Journey Across Two Continents.*[5]

The emergence of the Soviet Union and then China as closed Communist societies during the twentieth century, combined with cheap sea and eventually air transport,

---

* Uncle of the famous 'Red Baron', World War 1 air ace. Oddly there is a connection between the Red Baron and the inventor of Bentley Cars, W.O. Bentley. Bentley, originally a railway engineer, became an aero engine maker in the First World War, making the engines for the Sopwith aeroplanes including the famous Sopwith Camel. The BR.I and BR.II Bentley Rotary engines powered British fighter planes, the BR.I being standard on the Sopwith Camel, the BR.II being the last of the rotary powerplants used by the RAF. Apparently W.O. Bentley and the Red Baron had encounters, albeit indirect ones, during World War 1. 'On a visit to the front, W.O. was strafed by Manfred von Richthofen, the Red Baron, who later died in aerial combat with Canadian flying ace Roy Brown. Cited in 'Bentley A Motoring Miscellany' by Nicholas Foulkes, W.O. said later, "I almost felt a pang of regret when Brown in a Camel, powered by one of our B.R.IIs, caught him at last."'

A further Baron von Richthofen became a family friend when he was the German Ambassador in the UK in the early 1990s when my father was Lord Mayor of London. Naturally, given his name, the Ambassador had some exciting moments with the British tabloid press of that time.

We discovered that putting stickers on cars was more difficult than we had expected. Thanks very much to Rowena and Ianthe who did it for us in Beijing.

Last-minute supplies for the rally purchased in Beijing.

Beijing's head of traffic police explained to us how to drive in China.

Don't brush your teeth with this – Mike cleaning the spark plugs with a wire brush.

The Great Wall Lion Dance with the wall in the background.

We are off…

The view from our
place in the revolving
restaurant in Hohhot
(before it moved).

The rally enters the Gobi Desert.

You have to choose one of these tracks – and they don't all go the same way!

One of the more scenic and easier mountain passes in the Gobi.

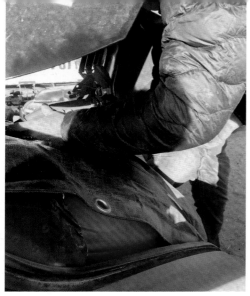

Fuelling the car from jerrycans at a campsite.

This was the point where our rally changed. We found a hole the size of a shoe in the lower fuel tank. Fortunately there was an upper fuel tank, and Mike and the sweeps are seen here linking up the upper tank to the fuel lines.

Cowboys and Indians? On the left is Mike's incredible tent – 'not a tent but an apartment!' – at Inkhet camp.

This statue of Genghis Khan, about 50km from Ulaanbaatar, is 40m high – 0.5 per cent of the world's population have his DNA!

Michael either enjoying a well-deserved lie-down on the rest day or more likely working pretty hard in Ulaanbataar.

We were lucky that this was one of the deepest streams we crossed – the Delgemoron River which can be close to impassable at certain times of year and in some places. One of the Alfas crossed upstream and sank.

Not the best start to the day at Undurkhangai Camp! And these tyres are meant to be guaranteed for 50,000km.

At least the colour of the duct tape matches – the Bentley in the car park at the upmarket Butlin's at Aya Lake.

The Altai Mountains in Siberia are very Swiss, except there is much more of them.

The front wheel falling off as we park in Novosibirsk – and after the Siberian mechanic had hand-made a replacement part.

After an 'interesting' stage in Siberia.

Fortunately the entrepreneurial Siberians generated a car wash about 10km onwards so that we could get hosed down!

eclipsed the Silk Roads until the late twentieth century. But the emergence of China as a major market and its voracious requirements for raw materials has created a new interest. In the last thirty years the Chinese have developed a major transport initiative, the Belt and Road Initiative, which will link the East with the rest of the world, particularly Central Asia and Western Europe. My consultancy Cebr has carried out the first major study of the economic impact of this which Mike and I launched in Beijing a week before the rally started.

The following section quotes from the report:

The study looks at the impact of the Belt and Road Initiative (BRI). The study uses Cebr's economic impact of transport and infrastructure analysis and Cebr's trade frictions analysis.

Although currently the BRI has about $2 trillion of projects already on the drawing board, we believe that as it succeeds it will expand to encompass many other projects. Ultimately over the next quarter century we expect it to involve as much as $8 trillion of spend.

We estimate that the Belt and Road Initiative is likely to boost world GDP by 2040 by $7.1 trillion per annum. This raises world GDP by 4.2 per cent of likely GDP in 2040 (or 8.3 per cent of GDP in 2019).

The benefits of the BRI are widespread. *As many as fifty-six different countries are forecast to have their annual GDP in 2040 boosted by more than $10 billion as a result of the project.*

Other than China, which by 2040 will be by far the world's largest economy and which will therefore benefit from any boost to the world economy, *the biggest single potential beneficiary of the BRI is (surprisingly) likely to be the US,* even though it isn't participating directly in the project. This is because of the sheer size of the US economy which means that it gains from the indirect effects of world GDP being boosted. Even though the boost to US GDP is only 1.4 per cent (much smaller than most other major economies) the absolute size of the US economy is still such that this is more than the absolute boost to any other economy except China. *The next largest impact is in Russia, followed by Japan, Indonesia, Korea, UK, India and the Netherlands.*

The region of the world that will most be transformed by the BRI is likely to be Central Asia and Russia where we predict that GDP in 2040 will be 18 per cent higher. GDP is also likely to be boosted in Central Europe (6 per cent), Western Europe (5 per cent) and East Asia (5 per cent).

The largest proportional impacts are in *Mongolia, the Kyrgyz Republic and Russia.*

Through the Belt and Road Initiative China will be continuing to drive world economic growth but in a different way from in the past. *In the ten years since the financial crisis in the West, China (now 15 per cent of the world economy) has driven world demand by accounting for 40 per cent of world GDP growth. Now looking forward China will be driving world GDP growth through helping the building of infrastructure throughout the world and through reducing both transport and other frictions that hold back world trade.*

The study also considers the impact that might emerge if the BRI is delayed for any reason, such as a world economic slowdown or because of technical difficulties. *If the spend is reduced by $1 trillion for example, world GDP (compared with the $2 trillion spend base case) will be reduced by $0.9 trillion or 0.5 per cent.* The region most affected will be Central Asia where GDP would be reduced by 5.9 per cent.

A key conclusion of the report is that *as the BRI develops, it is likely to attract in further countries.* Indeed it is highly likely that Western Europe, which has largely stayed aloof so far, will join in as the project develops momentum. It is even possible, though clearly unlikely under the current administration, that the US will also get involved in the BRI. But this is a longer term aspiration.

The World's Largest Infrastructure Project

A vital part of the Roman Empire was its transport links. Over the period 450 BCE to 150 CE the Romans built 382 great roads over their empire.[6] The length of the road network built by the Romans is estimated to have stretched to 400,000 kilometres of which 80,000 kilometres were paved.[7]

There has been no systematic attempt to build a complete network of interconnected infrastructures covering ranges of countries since then until now, although of course there have been plans linking small numbers of countries.

The earliest Roman road was the Via Appia, which was started (and finished) in 312 BCE. The first part joined Rome with Capua and was considered critical in enabling the Romans to subdue the Etruscans and the Samnites. The road was extended to Brindisium (modern-day Brindisi) in 264 BCE.

The Roman road network was largely completed before the Christian era, though some more were built in the first century AD. We have not made an estimate to cost the Roman road network but at today's prices a kilometre of non-motorway road costs at least $5–$10 million, so the network of 80,000 kilometres of paved roads might have cost up to $800 billion were it built today.

The Chinese Belt and Road project extends far beyond road infrastructure. It includes rail, energy, special development zones and urban transport systems. Eventually it will almost certainly become more electronic than purely physical as roads are upgraded for autonomous vehicles and as digital infrastructure becomes part of the system. The projects identified so far will cost about $2 trillion but many more will follow.

The road parts of the project have been estimated to comprise 60,000 kilometres of new or upgraded roads by the Mercator Institute for China Studies in Berlin. So the road part is actually smaller than the Roman road system.

But the most impressive aspect of the BRI is the combination of global reach and the speed with which it will come into effect. Most of the BRI system will be in place by 2040, implying a speed of building more than ten times faster than the Romans.

More interesting than the differences between the two systems are the similarities. The key point of the BRI is not just the physical and electronic infrastructure but the extent to which it makes trade around the world easier. The Roman roads were initially built for military reasons but eventually mainly existed to support and enhance trade.

Because the BRI is so critical to the world economy, it is important to understand how it is likely to affect this economy and where.

We have used two techniques to estimate this impact. The first is to use Cebr's techniques for estimating how improved infrastructure boosts productivity.[8] The second is work developed using agent-based modelling by Cebr to show how trade frictions affect trade and how reducing them can lead to substantial benefits to the world economy.[9] We have then fed the microeconomic results into Cebr's World Economic League Table Macroeconomic Model to derive the results for the global impact of the BRI on the world economy.

What We Have Compared

The Belt and Road Initiative (BRI) involves infrastructure development and investments and other potential changes including special economic zones and reduced customs formalities in

152 countries and international organizations in Asia, Europe, Africa, the Middle East, and the Americas.[10] 'Belt' refers to the routes for road *and* rail transportation, called 'the Silk Road Economic Belt'; whereas 'road' refers to the sea routes, or the twenty-first-century Maritime Silk Road.[11]

We have carried out a rigorous investigation of those BRI projects that have reached drawing board stage and identified 215 projects so far of varying size and importance. Our Energy and Transport teams have made a rough costing of these and they amount to a potential spending of about $2 trillion.

Clearly this is just the tip of the iceberg.

Our engineers have also looked at the discussions surrounding the BRI and have identified a wide range of additional projects that seem likely to link with the BRI.

Additional BRI areas are likely to include:

- A 5G global fibre network with global satellite cover.
- A global energy interconnector. See Geidco.org for many more details.
- Development of the Arctic Belt and Road where the Russian and Chinese initiatives will probably merge. Nordic and other countries will become involved.
- The Western European end of the Belt and Road – at present, other than Greece and the recent accession of Italy, Western Europe has stayed aloof. This is likely to change as the success of the Belt and Road Initiative

becomes more apparent – we believe it is highly likely that much of the rest of Europe will get involved including the UK, the Netherlands, Germany and France in particular. Also some more Central European countries like Poland.

- The autonomous vehicle Belt and Road – upgrading of the highways links to cater for autonomous vehicles.
- The hyperloop Belt and Road – a worldwide network of hyperloop links.
- The green Belt and Road – a worldwide network of renewable energy sources and (most importantly) storage.
- The Pacific and Latin American Belts and Roads which will be improved transport and ports facilities including the tunnel through the Andes.
- An academic Belt and Road initiative that links universities and scientific research with potential long-term impacts on technology and productivity.

We have provisionally allocated $8 trillion of spend by 2040 on this for our evaluation. We have compared this with the base case which is the $2 trillion of spend already on the drawing board.

We have also looked at the implications if for various reasons the Belt and Road Initiative has to be scaled back or slowed down. This might happen if, for example, a global economic crisis reduces the appetite for taking on debt or if the technological difficulties of such an extensive and path-breaking set of projects turn out to be greater than anticipated. Our risk case assumes that the base case $2 trillion spend by 2040 is cut back to a spend of only $1 trillion. It is worth noting that even that level of spending would be greater than our estimate of the cost of building the 80,000 kilometres of paved Roman roads at today's costs.

BRI and Geopolitics

The Belt and Road Initiative has emerged at an interesting time for the world economy. Since 1890 the US has been the world's largest economy and indeed in the middle of the twentieth century, with much of the rest of the developed world ravaged by war, US GDP reached an astonishing 50 per cent of world GDP on some measures.

But, according to the latest Cebr World Economic League Table, in 2032 China will overtake the US to become the world's largest economy again. History tells us that such shifts in economic power do not occur without tensions. Moreover, as the Western world gradually diminishes in relative economic power, it is likely that a third mega power, India, with a population 50 per cent larger than China's by then, will also be amongst the leaders by the end of the twenty-first century.

Some critics see the BRI as an attempt by China to extend its influence and soft power. Cebr's view is that it is not surprising that a major world economy should wish to help encourage the rest of the world to develop. Since our calculations suggest that the impact is positive for world GDP we see it as a win–win for the other world economies. We also see the BRI as a welcome antidote to the impact of the trade tensions currently surrounding the world economy.

We expect those parts of the world that are currently less enthusiastic about the BRI to become more so as it starts to show its benefits. We attach a high probability to Western Europe joining in much more closely than hitherto and it seems possible (though clearly not under the current Trump administration) that if some rapprochement between the US and China takes place that the US will also eventually join in with the initiative.

Who Is Impacted?

We have estimated the impact on world GDP in 2040.

The full Belt and Road is likely to boost world GDP by 2040 by $7.1 trillion per annum. This raises world GDP by 4.2 per cent of likely GDP in 2040 (or 8.3 per cent of GDP in 2019). In other words world GDP growth between now and 2040 is predicted to be boosted by 0.2 per cent per annum. This is a massive increase and reflects not only the scale of the infrastructure but its particularly significant impact in boosting trade and leveraging the potential gains from trade around the world. We are assuming that the effects of the improved infrastructure are matched proportionately by other measures to facilitate trade including improved border procedures in addition to the special economic development zones that are already part of the BRI project.

The key results of the study are set out in Table 2. It isn't surprising that China, sponsor of the project, is the biggest beneficiary. What is much more surprising, given the opposition to BRI from the current US administration, is that the second largest beneficiary in absolute terms is the US! This is because the US is such an important part of the world economy that it is impossible to boost the world economy without there being an effect on the US through its impact on US exports and through its multipliers.

Table 2: Top Fifty Countries Gaining Most in Absolute Terms from the BRI

GAINS BY COUNTRY FROM THE BRI IN 2040 $ BILLIONS ANNUAL RATE		
CHINA	EAST ASIA	1,777
UNITED STATES	NORTH AMERICA	402
RUSSIA	CENTRAL ASIA	377
JAPAN	EAST ASIA	282
INDONESIA	EAST ASIA	267
KOREA	EAST ASIA	219
UNITED KINGDOM	WESTERN EUROPE AND SCANDINAVIA	178
INDIA	SOUTH ASIA	173
NETHERLANDS	WESTERN EUROPE AND SCANDINAVIA	132
PAKISTAN	SOUTH ASIA	117
AUSTRALIA	PACIFIC	93
TURKEY	CENTRAL AND EASTERN EUROPE	91

GAINS BY COUNTRY FROM THE BRI IN 2040 $ BILLIONS ANNUAL RATE		
GERMANY	WESTERN EUROPE AND SCANDINAVIA	80
THAILAND	EAST ASIA	78
BRAZIL	LATIN AMERICA AND THE CARIBBEAN	73
ITALY	WESTERN EUROPE AND SCANDINAVIA	69
DENMARK	WESTERN EUROPE AND SCANDINAVIA	67
MALAYSIA	EAST ASIA	66
SPAIN	WESTERN EUROPE AND SCANDINAVIA	66
CHILE	LATIN AMERICA AND THE CARIBBEAN	63
SWEDEN	WESTERN EUROPE AND SCANDINAVIA	62
SINGAPORE	EAST ASIA	55
FRANCE	WESTERN EUROPE AND SCANDINAVIA	54
POLAND	CENTRAL AND EASTERN EUROPE	48
ARGENTINA	LATIN AMERICA AND THE CARIBBEAN	43
ISLAMIC REPUBLIC OF IRAN	MIDDLE EAST AND NORTH AFRICA	43
CANADA	NORTH AMERICA	35
NEW ZEALAND	PACIFIC	34
MYANMAR	EAST ASIA	33
VIETNAM	EAST ASIA	32
NIGERIA	SUB-SAHARAN AFRICA	30
UKRAINE	CENTRAL AND EASTERN EUROPE	28
BANGLADESH	SOUTH ASIA	24
COLOMBIA	LATIN AMERICA AND THE CARIBBEAN	23
ROMANIA	CENTRAL AND EASTERN EUROPE	22
PERU	LATIN AMERICA AND THE CARIBBEAN	22
KAZAKHSTAN	CENTRAL ASIA	20
MONGOLIA	EAST ASIA	19
CAMBODIA	EAST ASIA	18
SERBIA	CENTRAL AND EASTERN EUROPE	18

GAINS BY COUNTRY FROM THE BRI IN 2040 $ BILLIONS ANNUAL RATE		
TAIWAN	EAST ASIA	17
CZECH REPUBLIC	CENTRAL AND EASTERN EUROPE	16
PAPUA NEW GUINEA	PACIFIC	16
KENYA	SUB-SAHARAN AFRICA	15
SAUDI ARABIA	MIDDLE EAST AND NORTH AFRICA	15
PHILIPPINES	EAST ASIA	15
NORWAY	WESTERN EUROPE AND SCANDINAVIA	13
HUNGARY	CENTRAL AND EASTERN EUROPE	13
SWITZERLAND	WESTERN EUROPE AND SCANDINAVIA	12
UNITED ARAB EMIRATES	MIDDLE EAST AND NORTH AFRICA	12

Other major beneficiaries are Russia, Japan, Indonesia, Korea, the UK, India and the Netherlands. But we have calculated that fifty-six countries will have their GDP boosted by more than $10 billion by 2040 as a result of the initiative.

In some ways more interesting are the countries that are set to be transformed in percentage terms by the Belt and Road Initiative. These are shown in Table 3.

The impact is largest in Mongolia, where opportunities for minerals extraction are opened up, the Kyrgyz Republic, which is affected in a similar way to Mongolia, and Russia, which is potentially massively affected by the new infrastructure, much of which in actual terms will be located there and which will become the major conduit between East and West. Pakistan, which is one of the largest direct beneficiaries in terms of actual Belt and Road projects, is also disproportionately affected.

Table 3: Countries with Biggest Percentage Impact on Economy from BRI

BRI IMPACT ON GDP IN 2040 %	
MONGOLIA	26.8
KYRGYZ REPUBLIC	18.1
RUSSIA	18.0
CAMBODIA	15.1
FIJI	13.0
MYANMAR	12.5
ECUADOR	12.1
PAKISTAN	11.4
UNITED ARAB EMIRATES	10.8
DENMARK	10.6
ZIMBABWE	10.5

The Global Construction Market

We have estimated that global construction spending in 2018 was $11,448 billion which represented 13.5 per cent of global GDP. We have previously forecast that this share, which is already one of the highest on record other than at times of post-war recovery, is likely to edge upwards for a range of reasons.

First, there is a wide range of mega projects underway, starting with the Chinese Belt and Road Initiative. These mega projects account for an increasing proportion of world GDP.

Second, in many economies there is an infrastructure backlog. In the coming years this will need to be made up so that planned GDP growth can take place.

Third, new technologies will require new investment in a wide range of construction activities.

Finally, with growth tailing off in the short term we are expecting governments around the world to boost growth with additional infrastructural spending.

But with the additional Belt and Road spending that is likely to be necessary to achieve the $8 trillion BRI plan envisaged, there will be even more construction spending than we had previously envisaged.

As a result we now project that construction spending will rise from $11.5 trillion to $29.4 trillion, or 16.6 per cent of world GDP, by 2033. Beyond that, it is likely that the electronics content of the BRI will rise disproportionately and so the construction share of world GDP is likely to stabilise or edge down.

The Risks

There are of course risks to this. There are the normal economic, political and military risks which always have to be taken into account.

But there are also risks that relate specifically to the projects themselves. They are at the cutting edge of technology and as a result who can tell what technological obstacles might emerge. Obviously there is an allowance for contingencies but who knows whether this will be sufficient.

There are also economic obstacles. If the world economy develops more slowly than expected, there is a risk that either lenders or borrowers might face debt obstacles which would constrain the pace of spending.

We have therefore considered a risk case where we have evaluated the impact of reducing the BRI spend by $1 trillion. The estimated impact of this is to reduce world GDP in 2040 by 0.5 per cent or $0.9 trillion. The region most affected is Central Asia, where GDP is reduced by 5.9 per cent.

Conclusions

These estimates are very tentative and of course are based on many assumptions. But what they show is that the Belt and Road Initiative is of worldwide importance and its impact, if successful, will be widespread.

As an economist, I was genuinely excited to be driving from China to Europe along a route that was very close to that of the planned infrastructure of the Belt and Road Initiative. It's only when you see the scale of the distances involved for yourself that you can fully appreciate how the Initiative is likely to change the world.

Much of Central Asia is laden with minerals. But because minerals are expensive to transport relative to their value in most cases, their exploitation is heavily dependent on the existence of good transport connections. We saw these connections being developed, occasionally literally in front of our eyes.

One felt a sense of being in at the beginning of the creation of a new world as this new infrastructure starts to change trade routes and to channel economic development in a different direction from hitherto.

4

THE BEST EVER GEOGRAPHY LESSON

One of the great advantages of the rally is what it teaches you at first hand about the geography of the Eurasian continent. Although travel across this continent was an important trade route for luxury goods until the sixteenth century, it had fallen into disuse in more recent years as seaborne trade grew. As a result the physical centre of the world, at least on the Mercator projection commonly used for atlases, had become economically almost an empty quarter.

But now, with the Belt and Road Initiative which was described in the previous chapter starting to be built, we seem to be at the beginning of a reinvigoration of this middle area of the world, in part due to the growth of the Chinese and Russian economies and in part due to the plans for infrastructure across the Eurasian continent. This chapter looks at some of the relevant economic history to put these changes into context.

For the past half millennium, the economic centre of the world has not been the geographic centre (at least on the Mercator projection) but the Atlantic Ocean. On the Eastern side have been the countries of Europe that 'discovered' the rest of the world in an astonishing burst of energy and creativity from the late 1490s onwards. The Museu de Marinha in Lisbon has a wonderful display including full-scale models of some of the ships that helped 'discover' the new world. The most astonishing fact about these is their size – they are all about the size of a small cabin cruiser of the type you might see cruising on the Thames. It must have been terrifying to brave the world's oceans in vessels that small. On the Western side has been the New World. The joint area has been responsible for the bulk of economic growth from just over 500 years ago until recently.

The 'Age of Discovery' (the word 'discovery' has to be placed in inverted commas because obviously the people living in these areas had already discovered these places) coincided with the industrialisation that led by 1951 to the 19 per cent of the world's population that lived in the West generating 57 per cent of the world's real GDP at purchasing power parity (and a very much higher share at market exchange rates).* This concentration of activity in the West was obviously an anomaly and was bound to become less prominent in time and I had the good fortune, being brought up in Asia from 1953, to be around on-site to see this process starting to take place, kickstarted by the extraordinary amount of spending in Asia resulting from the Vietnam War. The next section on the Great Divergence is adapted from my book *The Inequality Paradox*.

---

* The data actually includes two Eastern economies in Australia and New Zealand but their share is sufficiently small not to do serious damage to the results.

THE GREAT DIVERGENCE

To understand the process that led to the reduction in the economic importance of the middle of the world on the Mercator projection it is worth looking at economic history starting before the Great Divergence between the West and the East.

The so-called Great Divergence led to the rise in power and economic significance of the West from 1500 AD to 1950.

The political scientist Samuel Huntington called the sharp widening of the gap in technology and incomes between a few selected European nations and subsequently some offshoots of these nations on the one hand and the rest of the world on the other 'The Great Divergence'.[12]

In 1450 a betting person would probably have been at least as likely to bet that Mughal India, China or the Ottoman Empire would grow rich and accelerate clear of the rest of the world as that the European countries would do so.

Because my parents lived in the Malaysian town of Malacca when I was a small boy, one of the historical figures who has always intrigued me is the Chinese admiral Cheng Ho (now in Pinyin normally called Zheng He) who, if he didn't discover Malacca (there was already a sultan when he first arrived), certainly did a lot to develop it. He visited Malacca at least five times on his seven great voyages (on one of which he might possibly have reached the Americas,* though professional historians think he only got as far as the Mozambique Channel). Probably Malacca's best museum is the Cheng Ho Cultural Museum.

In Cheng Ho's time, China seemed the most technologically advanced nation in the world and his ships were many times larger (his biggest ships were about 400 feet long and 180 feet wide, compared with Columbus' flag ship the *Santa Maria*, which was 60 feet long and about 20 feet wide!) and many times more advanced than those in which the great Spanish, Italian and especially Portuguese navigators 'discovered' the world half a century later. Chinese nutritional standards and life expectancy were also significantly higher than those in Europe.

Meanwhile, during the fifteenth century, the Ottoman Empire conquered Constantinople, besieged Vienna, fought the Battle of Lepanto, captured Hungary and raided Moscow as well as conquering many parts of Central and Eastern Europe. Technologically it also looked well ahead of the European nations who were hard pressed to hold it off militarily.

---

* This is the theory presented by the interesting but amateur historian Gavin Menzies in his bestselling book *1421: The Year China Discovered the World.*

THE WEST PUSHING AHEAD

So why did Europe get ahead?

One of the most readable accounts of the Great Divergence is that of the former BBC economics correspondent Peter Jay.[13] One of the reasons that Peter Jay writes so well about the voyages of discovery is that he is himself, as well as a distinguished economist, a highly competent sailor who has personally undertaken epic voyages (including returning from his stint as UK Ambassador in the US by sailing across the Atlantic himself in a race). Jay puts the development of the world economy into a variant of an Hegelian pattern (action, reaction, synthesis) where man is ever questing for knowledge unless blocked.

In this perspective the Great Divergence emerges as a result of the competition for ideas spurred by the Reformation (a slight problem for me, having been brought up as a Catholic in various Jesuit monasteries!). The Reformation meant that Europe was testing different ideas about progress while the more rigid systems of belief (combined with a condescending attitude towards business and making money) of the Chinese and the Muslim empires as well as the parts of Europe that remained most heavily Catholic inhibited the thirst for knowledge and hence economic progress.[14]

Indeed the arrival of French Huguenots in Holland and England was a major spur to growth. Ironically, the latest wave of immigrants to London today working in Spitalfields and the area around, the same area colonised by the Huguenots, have created the new 'Flat White Economy' which has done so much to push the UK economy forward in the past ten years.[15]

Trade was considered by the Confucians as 'unproductive, uncultured and preoccupied with profit rather than the good of society'[16] – they obviously hadn't yet made the discovery of Adam Smith's invisible hand, which shows how one person's pursuit of profit can (under the right conditions) lead to the good of society.

Exploitation of the New World and, sadly, of slaves from Africa were also probable contributory factors to the Great Divergence. If we ever think of ourselves in the West as somehow intrinsically superior to other peoples, it is sobering to think of the deception and violence from the Western societies that accompanied these processes. Although many others might have behaved just as badly had they had the resources to do so, it remains a fact that the West did have the resources and did initiate this violence and deception.

The persistent warfare in Europe during most of the next 300 years, from 1500 on, arguably stimulated technological developments as well. It certainly helped develop weapons technology which enabled European nations to conquer and colonise much of the world.

Eventually the growth in per capita incomes created a world with a sufficient surplus over subsistence to finance an industrial take-off. The combination of technology and capital generated the industrial revolution which took over the UK in the nineteenth century and which was rapidly copied by the other European nations.

Much of the technology of the industrial revolution was contributed by my fellow Scots.[17] The Scottish Education Act of 1496 made it compulsory for sons of barons and substantial freeholders to be educated in grammar schools. From 1560 education was encouraged as a result of the Scottish Reformation. For people to be enlightened they needed to be able to read so that they could read the Bible. In 1696 the Scottish Parliament passed its 'Act for Settling of Schools', making it compulsory for each kirk (parish) to have a school. Thus education in Scotland at an early stage in history was widespread throughout society, creating a sufficient breadth of ideas and knowledge for people doing manual jobs. The mix of education and practical manual jobs provided the engineering knowledge that made the Scots of the era such great inventors.

In most other countries the people who were educated did not work with their hands and so, unlike the Scots, were generally unable to apply their education to artisan processes. Thomas Telford, the great engineer, was a stonemason originally but his mix of practical building knowledge and his education, which was not much more than most Scots of his era achieved, turned him into someone who could change the face of a nation.[18] The experience of Scotland from this time and indeed that of émigré Scots in the US, Canada, Australia and New Zealand is powerful support for the theory that the most important means of securing equality is education.

One of the consequences of the Great Divergence was a massive increase in inequality, especially between countries. Even poor people in rich countries were typically much better off than the bulk of the population of poorer countries.

The industrial revolution – despite fears to the contrary, which led to the Luddite rebellion of 1811–15 and the breaking of machines[19] – in fact created more jobs than it destroyed (though real wages of manual workers fell in the UK in the early part of the nineteenth century – both the two series commonly available show drops of around 25 per cent).[20] These declines in wages were reversed during the second half of the nineteenth century.

GLOBALISATION AND ASIA CATCHING UP

I had got excited about globalisation while I was being brought up in Malaysia. It is hard for someone who was not in Southeast Asia through the third quarter of the twentieth century to comprehend the scale of the change in living standards that took place in the country during that period. Between 1953 and 1976, when my family lived in Malaysia, per capita GDP in the country more than doubled from $1,440 to $2,910 despite rapid population growth.[21] And since the early 1970s, living standards in Malaysia have quadrupled according to one of the world's foremost experts on living standards and inequality, Martin Ravallion.[22]

What this meant was that conditions in the country changed from the majority of people living below the breadline (or in their case the rice equivalent) to living with some minor creature comforts. Bicycles had become widespread during the 1950s and early 1960s. In the late 1960s and early 1970s small motorcycles started to flood the roads. By the 1980s the motorcycles had been replaced by cars, creating the epic traffic jams that are now so characteristic of the Far East.

In the early 1970s in the East economic growth really started to take off with offshore manufacturing of electronic components. Asia in the 1950s and 1960s was mainly thought of economically as a producer of commodities and very cheap basic goods. In 1968 that changed. The electronics company Fairchild made the first offshore electronics investment in Hong Kong. I have a personal view which has been rarely mentioned in the literature (the main study on this is in Korean, though it has now been translated!) that the Vietnam War was catalytic in causing the first investments in East Asia.[23] Young American soldiers were drafted into the war and sent to Asia. I'm sure that their unusual experience abroad in Asia (remember at that time that very few Americans of their generation ever left the US) might have influenced their attitude to investment in East Asia when they returned to civilian life and made business decisions.

The peak level of annual expenditure by the US on Vietnam was (coincidentally) also in 1968 when, according to the Congressional Research Service, $111 billion was spent on the war, which they have helpfully translated into $738 billion at FY2011 dollars and about $840 billion in today's money.[24] As Senator Everett Dirksen pointed out, 'a billion here, a billion there, pretty soon you're talking about real money.' Eight hundred and forty billion dollars is real money and had already started to leach into the domestic Asian economies in the provision of basic supplies before Fairchild came in and started to make electronics products in Hong Kong.

We talk these days of wars creating 'collateral damage', which I feel is a nastily sanitised phrase to describe the killing of innocent people which often occurs during a war. But there are occasionally also 'collateral benefits', such as the stimulus given to economic development in East Asia.

When I was studying for my Master's at Oxford in 1972–74, the phenomenon of offshore electronics manufacturing in Asia already seemed to be developed enough for me to choose for my thesis to perform a cost–benefit analysis of the first two electronics plants in the Kuala Lumpur area. My thesis showed how massively they benefitted all parties.[25]

The first of them took a year to pay back its entire investment. The second took ten months. Employees working in the plants typically trebled their living standards from what they had been previously.

At the same time, even though the plants were in tax-free zones, government revenue was boosted strongly by income taxes, employment taxes and indirect taxes on the employees' expenditure. Incidentally, this is why I am careful not to confuse companies who pay little or no corporate taxes with companies paying no tax at all. While I think companies should pay a reasonable amount of corporate tax, their main contribution to the overall tax take is through their sales taxes and employees' taxes. Direct corporate tax payments on profits tend to be relatively unimportant in comparison and if low rates of corporate taxes promote economic growth, the government tax take is likely to gain much more than it loses from the lower tax rates.[26]

This offshore manufacturing was clearly going to transform those medium-income developing countries that took it up, like Hong Kong, Singapore, Taiwan, Thailand and Korea as well as Malaysia. It would transform the world economy as well as the countries in which the manufacturing was taking place when countries like China and India (who between them make up nearly two fifths of the world's population) emulated them.

But what we saw starting to happen in Malaysia and Hong Kong and also in Taiwan, Korea, Thailand and especially Singapore was an important economic theme of the 1970s and 1980s, though because these economies were still relatively small, the impact on the global economy remained muted.

These Asian countries plus Taiwan accounted for 3.2 per cent of the world economy in 1870 and were about the same percentage, 3.3 per cent, in 1970. Their share rose to a peak of 8 per cent in 1997 before the Asian currency crisis. The rise was very rapid but despite this, the net impact on the scale of the world economy was limited. China alone today is around 15 per cent of the world economy.*

Let me digress for a short time to deal with Japan. Japan was the first East Asian economy to industrialise. The Meiji Restoration in 1868 led to a process that allowed Japan to catch up with the Western economies. Japan's standard of living doubled between 1870 and the First World War, doubled again by 1939 and after a major slump during the war – much more than in most of the other belligerent countries – had recovered its pre-war level by 1956 and caught up with Western Europe by 1973.

Japan is an outlier. It was the only Asian economy to industrialise so early. Although it had scale, with a population which reached 100 million in 1967, and its industrialisation was distinctly faster than for Western Europe, nevertheless its

---

* All the numbers for the world economic history used here are from the Maddison Data Archive at the Groningen Growth and Development Centre at Groningen University in the Netherlands. Angus Maddison was a major scholar whose life work was in producing historically comparable data. His series cover world GDP, population and GDP per capita and go back to the year 1 CE. The figures are calculated in Geary–Khamis dollars at 1990 prices. This is essentially a purchasing power parity measure. This is appropriate for the historical data for periods when market exchange rates often did not exist or were unrepresentative.

total impact on the world economy was still relatively minor because it represented just one country.

Japan's share of world GDP rose from 2.3 per cent in 1870 to 8.7 per cent at its peak in 1991, which is non-trivial but still not enough on its own to mark a qualitative shift in things like world demand for resources.

There are two other reasons why Japan has been (other than in the Second World War) less disruptive. First, the speed of industrialisation – though rapid – has been about half that of East Asia and China. The second is that post-World War 2, the US has had the power to influence Japanese economic policy, so the Japanese have been forced to allow the yen to appreciate to reflect its competitiveness. So the super-competitive conditions that we have seen elsewhere only existed for a short period before the appreciation of the yen changed the position.

But Japan has been important in the story of the revival of Asia. First, it is hard to believe now, but as recently as a century ago, many people thought that industrialisation was somehow the preserve of the white races only. Japan's development to Western levels of prosperity conclusively proved that this was not the case. And of course, Japan's actions in the Second World War, though ultimately self-defeating, spelt the end of the Western, especially British, empires in the East.[27]

The examples of the emerging economies in East Asia as well as that of Japan were bound to affect other Eastern economies. With Taiwan and Hong Kong on their doorstep, one would have had to be immensely obtuse or blinded by ideology not to realise in China that Chinese people everywhere except in mainland China seemed to be doing remarkably well, while those in China were not. And once Chairman Mao had died, the new Chinese leadership was not obtuse or blinded by ideology. From the mid-1970s onwards they decided to copy what was being done in the economies on their doorstep.

In the 1960s President Johnson used to defend the actions of the US in Vietnam by talking about what he called the Domino Theory – that if one country fell to Communism it would knock over its neighbour country.

In the end, what happened was the Domino Theory in reverse. The economic success of East Asia changed China, which was one of the factors leading to President Gorbachev wanting to reform Russia and which over time was one of the factors that led to the fall of the Iron Curtain. I remember once explaining to Lee Kuan Yew, the eminent Singaporean leader, that he had caused the fall of the Iron Curtain – he was amused by the idea, though he was less amused when I explained that the previous time I had visited Singapore as a rebellious teenager in transit to Kuala Lumpur I had been kept in preventative detention at the airport because my hair was too long.

And of course we are not just talking about these economies alone. Latin America saw which way the wind was blowing and changed course, although some parts have since changed course again and gone into retreat. More importantly, other emerging economies in Africa and Asia, of which the most important was India, also began to change.

A coincidental factor that was hugely important in all this was the emergence of information and communications technology. The new electronic technologies created a mass demand for cheap mass-produced electronic components and products which have been the main driving technology for East Asian economic development. They have also reduced the tyranny of location and allowed businesses throughout the world to enter into the software industry. This has been especially important for India, since it allowed Indian software exports to escape the so-called Permit Raj that had – very much with the help of the professors of economic development – done so much to slow down India's emergence from the economic doldrums.

The effects of globalisation have been to remove the Western world's dominance of the production of economically sophisticated goods. This has meant in turn that ordinary workers in the Western world have lost their jobs or been forced to accept a squeeze in their living standards. Note that this does not mean that had the West put up protectionist barriers to this trade they could have avoided the squeeze. The squeeze has resulted also from changed terms of trade. Protection would not have helped the West improve its terms of trade by much and would have come at a cost in lost economic growth, which also would have weakened the position of the worst off in the Western world.

THE TRANSFORMATION OF RUSSIA

As explained above, the process that led to the Chinese economic reforms and China's emergence on the world stage also affected Russia. In the first instance this led to a fairly chaotic series of privatisations, handing over corporations to the so-called oligarchs.

Under President Putin, things changed. Although he clearly has been pretty dictatorial and there are questions about the extent of the rule of law, he does appear gradually to be moving the country towards a more stable internal policy. The Peking Paris rally obviously has to go through Russia, but in 2016 the organisers tried to minimise the extent to which it did. In 2019 we spent a lot of time – about three weeks – in Russia and most of us on the rally were very impressed with the extent of the changes.

First and most important, at no point was anyone held up by gangsters. One participant had her handbag taken from an unlocked car at a service station. Otherwise no crime on any of the ralliers was reported. On previous occasions gangsters had held up ralliers at road blocks and tried to extort as much as $10,000.

Second, we saw little evidence of petty crime. At one hotel there was a strip club in the basement and I was told by someone who went in out of curiosity that it was just a clip joint. But otherwise no one preyed on us and we felt quite safe. (Ironically we felt much more on edge in the next country, Finland, where the traffic cops have quite an aggressive reputation.)

Third, widespread drunkenness seems to be a thing of the past. Obviously everywhere we stopped in the Bentley we were the centre of attention, particularly from the local truck drivers for whom we provided a high point in what otherwise could be a fairly boring day. They all crowded round and asked to be photographed with us. And at no point did we smell alcohol on anyone's breath. Those who had been on the rally through Russia in the past said that this was an amazing change. And the official statistical data backs this up – life expectancy in Russia was 64.4 years in 1994 and is now 71.9 years (2018).[28] Clearly there has been a transition to a less unhealthy lifestyle. The drink driving laws are pretty draconian. In theory any alcohol at all in one's blood means arrest and loss of licence. This certainly made us careful with how many beers we risked the night before if we were driving the next day.

Finally, the roads in Russia seem to have caught up with the West. Very rarely were they potholed or badly maintained. Six years ago on the rally, a participant had been killed when a driver had allegedly fallen asleep and careered across the road into their path. According to press reports:

[T]he police were investigating eyewitness reports that the driver of the Polo had 'fallen asleep at the wheel moments before careering across the road into the path of the oncoming Chevrolet'.

'There were no skidmarks and traffic was very light,' she [the eyewitness] said.

The BBC's Moscow correspondent, Daniel Sandford, said the long and poorly maintained stretch of road was notorious for car accidents and was described locally as 'the road of death'.[29]

The Foreign Office briefing on Russia which I attended before the rally explained a certain amount of what has changed in Russia in recent years.

First, it appeared that although President Putin remained the public face of the administration, much of the actual running of the country had been handed over to his prime minister and long-time close associate Dmitry Medvedev. Medvedev, who first came to prominence as chairman of the Russian energy company Gazprom, has worked with President Putin for a long time, even swopping jobs with him when term limits forced Putin to step down as president temporarily. He has had an academic career and is generally considered much more technocratic than Putin.

Second, Medvedev appears to have brought in groups of young (under thirty-five-year-old) technocrats to run the country internally. This has made the running of cities and other local areas much more efficient and much less corrupt.

Third, the economy is transforming itself from being based purely on natural resources to a much more skill-based economy, particularly in IT. There are markets on the internet where you can tender for IT work worldwide. The data from these markets suggests that there are more than 700,000 enterprises selling bits of software or more to the UK alone. I'm sure that very little of this gets properly recorded in the GDP statistics.

Meanwhile, Russia is powering up the world league tables for educational success and currently ranks as high as fourth[30] and is indicating much more activity in e-commerce than hitherto. A recent IMF report showed that the share of e-commerce in Russian imports had risen from an average of 2.5 per cent in 2016 to 4.2 per cent for Q1 2017.[31] One of the consequences of this is that internally Russia is setting itself up to perform much better in the future than in the past. Increasingly its skills are modern as it moves up the educational league table and its infrastructure is also catching up.

Fourth, the country is upgrading its infrastructure. This was noticeable throughout the Russian part of the rally but was especially obvious as we drove around and past St Petersburg, where the roads and bridges looked much better than those in most of Western Europe.

If you drive across the whole of a country as big as Russia you get quite a thorough impression of how their economy is doing and how their popular culture is developing. And while it is certainly true that there are plenty of groups who have been left behind, there are also plenty of groups who are becoming essentially Western in their behaviour, living standards and lifestyle.

This is in sharp contrast to the impression given in the Western media who have tended, partly because of political disputes, to treat Russia as if it remained in the dark ages. My impression is that the media often tends to base its assessments of countries on how they treat journalists. In the past there was a degree of correlation between pace of economic progress and freedom of speech, and this might return in the future if growth becomes more dependent on software and creativity. But we currently seem to be in an intermediate stage of economic and political development where it is possible up to a point to generate substantial economic progress even under politically repressive regimes. And it is important to be factually based in one's analysis and not assume that just because a regime has political features that one dislikes, it must be failing economically.

Of course many whose political views are right of centre in the West feel that the media is biased against them.[32] It is important, though, not to equate any media bias in the West, which to the extent it exists probably reflects groupthink and the lack of practical real-world experience by journalists, with the locking up and murdering of journalists in other societies.

And there are many Western journalists who still are prepared to report and give airtime to others with different views from their own, though their number seems to be diminishing.

Another reason why the West has failed to understand the scale of the change taking place in Russia is the bad reputation that the behaviour of Russians abroad gives the country. Quite apart from the killings of oligarchs and others, many Westerners associate Russians with loud and unpleasant behaviour, with bullying and unreliability. I admit myself that before driving across Russia I had shared these views, partly based on my own observation of Russians in St John's Wood High Street and elsewhere. So it was a surprise to see that Russians in Russia behaved with considerable circumspection. For example, in traffic jams, most Russians patiently waited their turn. It was interesting that those who tried to push in were generally driving dark-windowed large 4x4 vehicles, very similar to those who drive so badly in St John's Wood.

One morning over breakfast on the rally Paul Polman, the Dutch business grandee who is ex-CEO of Unilever and ex-CFO of Nestlé, said, 'Douglas, you know, the Russian GDP data must be understated.' I agreed with him. This is partly because the digital sectors of economies are very hard to measure and so countries like Russia, with a fast-growing digital sector, almost always understate GDP. Before I visited Russia I had suspected that GDP was overstated. Having driven across the country I now agree with Paul Polman that the opposite is probably the case.

Moreover, it looks as if the Russian economy is poised for a further leap forward as its digital economy develops, partly based on the educational and infrastructural improvements that have already occurred, in addition to the future improvements that are planned.

THE SCALE OF RUSSIA

What is hard to imagine about Russia without driving through it is how huge it is. Table 4 shows how large it is, pretty well twice the size of any other country, covering 11 per cent of the entire world's land mass. Of the thirty-six days we spent on the rally, more than half were spent in Russia. Because of its size Russia is a country like no other.

One interesting aspect of Russia can be seen in the railways. The basic rule of thumb for transport planning is that because of transhipment costs, rail is uneconomic for freight for distances below 200 kilometres, though transport strategists are trying to change this. So in most of Western Europe rail is used much more heavily for transporting people than freight.

But of course in Russia 200 kilometres is a tiny distance. And while you might want to travel by rail as a passenger for the same reason as we were travelling by car – for the views

Table 4: The World's Top Ten Countries by Land Mass

	COUNTRY	SQ KMS	SQ MILES	OF WORLD'S LAND MASS
1	RUSSIA	16,376,870	6,323,142	11.0
2	CHINA	9,388,211	3,624,807	6.3
3	UNITED STATES	9,147,420	3,531,837	6.1
4	CANADA	9,093,510	3,511,022	6.1
5	BRAZIL	8,358,140	3,227,095	5.6
6	AUSTRALIA	7,682,300	2,966,151	5.2
7	INDIA	2,973,190	1,147,955	2.0
8	ARGENTINA	2,736,690	1,056,641	1.8
9	KAZAKHSTAN	2,699,700	1,042,360	1.8
10	ALGERIA	2,381,740	919,595	1.6

and the experience – you would not normally travel that way as a passenger if you were simply trying to get somewhere. So in Russia, one of the first things I learned about rail was that it is primarily a mode for transporting freight.

In Luigi Barzini's book about driving across Tsarist Russia in the original Peking to Paris event in 1907 it is clear that the very scale of the country affected its administration. In the days before communication was highly developed, local bosses – whether industrial or political – had few constraints on their behaviour other than extreme reactions if central authority felt affronted. Permissions to progress in the rally were clearly subject to local whims and one would guess that a traveller with less than Prince Borghese's rank would have found it far more difficult to get the permissions necessary at a local level to travel across the country.

ARE RUSSIA AND CHINA COMING TOGETHER?

It was always likely that in a world where the US was led by President Trump and where the EU had little military weight and was suffering economically, Russia and China would become more closely aligned.

But the development of infrastructure linking the two is pushing this alignment more rapidly than might otherwise be the case. The increasing trade and other economic links are likely to accelerate the development of political links between the two countries.

Russia has its own version of the Belt and Road Initiative, called the Greater Eurasian Partnership. This seems to have as an objective the increase of trading links between Europe, especially Russia, and Asia. There are two aspects of this. First, the Eurasian Economic Union, which came into being in 2015 and links Belarus, Kazakhstan, the Kyrgyz Republic and Armenia with Russia. This economic union, modelled on the EU, has definite substance – as we noticed when crossing the Russian–Kazakh border twice, where the border crossings held us up for minutes only rather than the multiple hours it took to cross from China into Mongolia and from Mongolia into Russia. The second leg of the Partnership is increased infrastructure to facilitate trade. Russia's longer-term aim seems to be to link its own initiative with the Chinese initiative. There seems little reason to assume that this will not happen.

When Russia and China were economically underdeveloped, their markets did not justify the cost of bringing infrastructure to a remote part of the world. But the development of China already has changed this. Amongst the spam I have received in my inbox recently is the following:

From: good@tech-inc.cn [mailto:good@tech-inc.cn]
On Behalf Of zfpl
Sent: 08 October 2019 06:01
To: Douglas McWilliams
Subject: China Europe Rail Transport 中欧铁路运输

Hi sir
This is rainy from china.
中国成都到欧洲铁路运输费用明细:

China Chengdu to Europe rail transportation costs:
FROM Destination USD/40HQ USD/20GP Transit Time

成都*Chengdu* 罗茨*Lodz*	2400 xxx 11days	
成都*Chengdu* 纽伦堡*Nuremberg*	1600 xxx 15days	
成都*Chengdu* 蒂尔堡*Tilburg*	2600 xxx 16days	
罗茨*Lodz* 成都*Chengdu*	600 xxx 16days	
纽伦堡*Nuremberg* 成都*Chengdu*	1600 xxx 16days	
蒂尔堡*Tilburg* 成都*Chengdu*	1800 xxx 18days	

另外还有中国到马拉，汉堡，杜伊斯堡，鹿特丹，伦敦等，
欢迎咨询。

*There are also Chinese to Mala, Hamburg, Duisburg,
Rotterdam, London, etc. Welcome to consult*

铁路把中国到欧洲的时间节省了50%的时间，费用仅仅是空
运的20-30%，加速货物运转，增加贸易效率。

*The railway saved 50% of the time from China to Europe.
The cost was only 30% of air freight, which accelerated
cargo operations and increased trade efficiency.*

I've checked with others and it does appear that this offer is
genuine. Amongst the interesting phenomena are the price
differentials – Chengdu–Lodz $2,400, Lodz–Chengdu $600.*
This confirms what I might have suspected, which is that many
of the wagons return to China empty. Shipping is still notice-
ably cheaper, but if the infrastructure speeds up and border
checks reduce, the land route is bound to grow in importance.

Russia and China are major powers with different interests, so there will always be a limit to the extent to which
they align their foreign policies. But the Sino-Soviet split in the
1960s and 1970s, which partly reflected rivalry for leadership

---

* Incidentally my friend and former CBI colleague Michael Deminiski who
runs the British Polish Chamber of Commerce from Warsaw has explained to
me that Lodz became a destination because Stalin, who built the key railway
infrastructure, wanted to keep it away from centres of population like Warsaw
to prevent sabotage.

of the Communist bloc and partly the hurt feelings of charismatic dictatorial leaders both used to getting their way, seems unlikely to be replicated.

Instead the future is likely to see increased alignment as the two powers are forced ever closer together by shared trade links, infrastructure and their geographical proximity.

IMPACT OF TRANSFORMED RUSSIA AND CHINA FOR THE COUNTRIES IN BETWEEN

Driving through Mongolia and Kazakhstan it was clear that they were about to be transformed by Belt and Road infrastructure.

Both are huge, with tiny populations. They seem full of minerals which will certainly, with the development of the end user markets in China especially but also elsewhere in Russia and Western Europe, justify the expense of the infrastructure that will go across them, linking them with both the East and the West.

Yet especially in Mongolia, this is likely to pose a challenge to their way of life. Both Mike and I thought that the children in Mongolia seemed the happiest we had ever seen. They appear to be allowed to run around as they wish (which is probably why they are happy!) They look well fed and healthy. But one wonders what the development of infrastructure and minerals exploitation will do for them. Parents working down mines are likely to have much less child-friendly hours than those engaged in desultory farming. Roads and mines will probably be fenced in and will limit the extent to which the children can go where they like. I have a sense that Mongolians particularly may become richer but less happy. Let's hope I'm wrong.

But it is hard not to see the present as at least the beginning of the end of an era for the lands in the middle of the world. They are currently largely empty of population, devoid of infrastructure and lack much economic activity. One suspects the coming years will change this and make the area much more developed and industrialised. It was great to drive through while it was in a relatively untouched state but one suspects that future ralliers and others will drive through a very different landscape.

5

THE RALLY, THE CARS
AND THE PEOPLE

THE RALLY

The history of the rally is nearly as exotic as the cars and participants.

In 1907 the newspaper *Le Matin* published a challenge in its issue of 31 January: 'What needs to be proved today is that as long as a man has a car, he can do anything and go anywhere. Is there anyone who will undertake to travel this summer from Peking to Paris by automobile?'

There were intended to be forty entrants but eventually only five teams took up the challenge, leaving from the French Embassy in Beijing. Four of these finished eventually (the entrant who didn't finish was driving a Mototri Contal tricycle, and this year two intrepid Belgians with a replica decided to try to complete the feat that their predecessor in 1907 had failed to achieve – see below). Refuelling stops were organised by sending camels ahead. The race followed a telegraph route and each participant took one journalist who filed news reports.

The winner was Prince Scipione Borghese, accompanied by his mechanic Ettore Guizzardi and the journalist Luigi Barzini (father of the better-known journalist of the same name), driving a huge Itala car with a 7.4-litre engine. Barzini wrote the story of the journey in the first of the Peking Paris books, *Peking to Paris: A Journey Across Two Continents*.

There were no more Peking to Paris rallies until after the modernisation of China and the break-up of the Soviet Union. Then a man called Philip Young, a motor rallying enthusiast, set up the Endurance Rally Association and managed to persuade the countries en route to allow the rally to take place. The official second Peking to Paris was held in 1997 (though a London to Beijing event was held in 1990).

The 2019 event was the seventh official such rally. It attracted 106 participants. The route was essentially similar to the 1907 route, going from Beijing to cross the Mongolian border at Erenhot, going through Ulaanbaatar for an initial rest day and then into Siberia for a well-earned rest and much more mechanical work in Novosibirsk. This year for the first time the rally entered Kazakhstan and veered through the capital Nur-Sultan (better known under its previous name as Astana) before going back into Russia, crossing the Urals and then following much of the course of the Volga River before reaching St Petersburg. Again new for the rally, we drove into Finland, visited Helsinki and then took a ferry to Tallinn in Estonia before crossing the Baltic states into Poland. After three days in Poland, two in Germany and a final two nights in Belgium we ended up in Paris.

THE CARS AND THE PEOPLE

There were some wonderful vehicles on the rally. It's worth describing a few.

First and most exotic, Car No 1, a Mototri Contal tricycle. This is a replica of one of the five vehicles that started the original 1907 rally and the only one that failed to finish after it fell down a ravine and disappeared without trace. The crew were lucky to survive when found, nearly starving, by locals. The driver in the 2019 rally, Anton Gonnissen, is an iron man. One of the other rally participants described him as the sort of man who, on finding that the city where he is spending his rest day is holding a marathon, decides immediately to run it. He needed all of his strength for the rally. In real life he is a successful architect. His navigator, Herman Gelan, an interior designer, also from Ghent, is more the strong silent type, but must be the bravest of the competitors. He was banned from Chinese motorways because of the inherent lack of safety of the design but, undeterred, flew to Hohhot and rejoined the rally where he met up with the tricycle and Anton.

I had a couple of beers with Anton and the builder of the replica tricycle in St Petersburg and it was immediately clear that this was a passion for him, and he showed me pictures on his phone of many other exotic replicas that he had created. He was only too delighted to share in his clients' success.

Car No 2 was nearly as exotic – a 1910 White MM steam car driven by Mitch Gross and Chris Rolph. By special dispensation they were allowed a team of mechanics to follow them. They needed at least one new engine during the rally and often terrified bystanders with the fires they set to get the car going. They claimed in the bar that the car worked best with 80-octane fuel 'or even better on kerosene', though I wasn't clear how much they meant it. Like Anton and Herman, they did well to make it to the end. This was also by far the biggest car on the event, at 25 feet long.

One of the nicest cars on the event, and certainly one of the most charming crews, was that of Miss Vicky, a 1931 Ford Model A Victoria from Seattle, which raised $30,000 to fight against polio, an amount that was tripled by the Bill and Melinda Gates Foundation. Lee Harman, an ex-eye surgeon, and Bill Ward, a special forces veteran, helped save our lives by giving us their spare fuel can when we holed our tank in Mongolia. Their car was beautifully turned out and showed the strength of US engineering in the 1930s. When my friends Rikkee Curtis and the Sultan of Selangor entered the rally for the first time in 1997 they had also driven a Model A and their experience testified to the car's basic suitability. Rod Wade and Kelly Whitton drove another Ford Model A which just seemed to keep on going.

Also helping to save our rally were Alan and Steve Maden from Melbourne, Australia. They, like us, had decided to see if they could make a luxury car complete the event and had built a very good rally car around their 1975 Rolls-Royce Silver Shadow. We posted quite similar times on the competitive sections, though they were often a second or so faster. They made the difference to us by lending us two 20-litre fuel bladders, without which we would not have made it through Mongolia. They were a lovely pair of people, though like many Aussies underneath the surface they were very competitive. Their car was a bit more modified than ours, with a cage strengthening the bodywork and adjustable suspension. But the inside of the car was left original in the front with the wood facings left as when new. We had great fun with them and even managed to have a kick around with them with our rugby ball, which was otherwise unused, while we were camping in Mongolia.

Also fun to be with were Nick Grewal and Dirk Burrowes from the US. We enjoyed their company a lot. Dirk, presenter of *Classic Drive TV* in the US, was the mechanical expert. Nick financed the expedition and drove, according to Dirk, aggressively. We got on with them from the moment we were placed close to them at the gala dinner on the first evening. Their car was a 1940 Packard, again a testimony to the early mid-twentieth-century American engineering robustness.

Mario Illien and his daughter Noele were about the most popular pair on the rally. Mario could have afforded to have a team of engineers flying behind him. But instead he diligently spent hours under the car himself keeping it in good shape. He and his late partner Paul Morgan had founded Ilmor Engineering, one of the most successful racing motor engine manufacturers of all time. Ilmor Engines won the Formula One World Championship three times before he sold out to Mercedes. The engine of the car in which Lewis Hamilton has just won his sixth world championship is based on his original engineering. And his engines have succeeded in winning at most other kinds of motor sport.

His daughter Noele has a very sweet nature and a great sense of humour. An apprentice journalist, she managed to get *The New York Times* to print an excellent article by her on the rally.[33] They drove a 'Maigret' Citroën which kept overtaking us, though at one point when our brakes had failed we overtook them too... I'm sure they didn't cheat with their tuning (why would they?) but they obviously knew how best to get power from their engine and managed a remarkable turn of speed. They were the car arriving in Paris immediately in front of us and like us had to turn the engine off in the traffic jam at the end of the rally and push the car over into the Place Vendôme.

Paul Polman and Daniel Spadini drove another Citroën, a DS, that also seemed often to be in the same part of the rally as us. Paul had just retired as CEO of Unilever, having been previously CFO of Nestlé. He has spoken often at Davos and elsewhere of how to make capitalism work better – his view is that financial predators have too much power. A lot of his thinking is similar to mine, as expressed in my last book *The Inequality Paradox: How Capitalism Can Work for Everyone*, although we propose different solutions. We enjoyed our talks over breakfast and elsewhere. Daniel is a real charmer and was by far the best-dressed man on the rally. He managed a freshly pressed long-sleeve shirt every day (on the last day he told me that the rally had to end that day 'because this is my last shirt').

After the rally I was having lunch with my favourite advertising man, Rory Sutherland, and I mentioned that one of the world's great marketing experts, Keith Weed, had also participated on the rally. It turned out that Rory was doing a one-day workshop with Keith the very next day and he invited me to appear – I nearly did. Keith has probably authorised more spending on advertising than anyone else in the world ever – he was head of marketing worldwide for Unilever and had a budget of $8 billion. I was interested that a company with so diverse a product range should have a centralised spend, but he explained to me that this was needed to negotiate good terms with the internet giants: 'They claim not to give discounts but... they do'. His co-driver Richard Holmes is a fellow economist and so we would occasionally indulge in intellectual sparring. They managed to turn their car, a rather attractive and well-prepared 1940 Pontiac, over on a lively part of the road in Mongolia but fortunately escaped, dented but unhurt. They also had engine problems, sorted by the arrival of a new engine in St Petersburg. Before that they were going through 12 litres of oil a day.

I was impressed at how so many of the ladies on the rally managed to present themselves so well. Many of us men became pretty ragged looking with beards and unkempt hair but all of the women made a huge effort to look smart. The effect added to the joy of the rest of us men, even if we failed to live up to the standards that they set. One of the more elegant ladies was Janel Trowbridge from Bozeman, Montana, who with her husband Mark rallied a most beautifully finished P1800 Volvo in a wonderful deep maroon. I may have been the only other person on the rally to have visited Bozeman, which I had done twice. In 1984, I was taken by the US State Department on a 'Young Leaders of the Future' tour arranged by the then economics attaché in the US Embassy in London, my good friend Barbara Bowie (now Bowie-Whitman, who kindly flew into Paris to be at the end of rally celebration). One of my hosts on that trip was the environmental economist Terry Anderson, then based in the University of Montana in Bozeman. Ianthe and I also visited Bozeman when we drove round the US in 2013 because it is one of the towns closest to Yellowstone National Park. Janel had trained as a ballet dancer and her elegant posture was part of her charm. Mark, much shorter than Janel, had fixed the seats of the car so she could not drive, and so she had to push when necessary. We started chatting to them in Beijing and found them good fun and great company for the duration of the rally.

The day before we picked up our cars for the rally we were looking for fuel additives and taken by the rally organisers to a sort of car city with about 400 shops selling different items for cars in southern Beijing. We eventually found the fuel additives (which turned out to be largely unnecessary) in about the fortieth shop in which we looked. We were taken with the two Belgian 'Dodge Brothers', two childhood friends from near Ypres in Belgium, Patrick Debussere and Bernard Vereenooghe, who were looking for a replacement battery. Patrick and Bernard were very much the life and soul of every party on the rally and eventually, when we stopped in the wonderful old market square in Ypres, gave all the participants in the rally the party to end all parties on behalf of the Belgian participants. They even issued tokens so that the drinks were free (though I'm not sure how much they enjoyed my joke that these beer tokens would become the new European currency when the euro broke up). They drove a beautiful 1933 Dodge convertible.

Also the life and soul of most parties were Nick Wade and Steve Borthwick, driving a 1940 Flathead Ford that looked very much like a refugee from a gangster movie. Their dynamo stopped working very early on and they kept going by trickle charging the battery every night. Obviously this left them with little ability to use any of the other electrical equipment on the car. They seemed to have about the same capacity for beer and wine as us and we spent many enjoyable evenings talking nonsense with them. Given the problems that they had with keeping the car going, we were particularly delighted that they made it to Paris. We have stayed in touch since the rally.

Paul Hickman and Bas Gross were driving an unpainted Bristol 403 for the second consecutive time on the rally. They were both good mechanics and on more than one occasion they generously gave us useful advice that helped fix something we had missed. Their car has since been painted a beautiful green and looks wonderful.

Graham and Marina Goodwin were fellow Bentley drivers in a 1925 Bentley Super Sports. They won the vintage category and showed themselves expert ralliers. Graham is also chairman of Rally the Globe, a new not-for-profit rally organisation. Their car was expertly prepared and they were clearly experienced rally drivers. We wish them luck in their new venture.

Most of my friends were surprised when I explained to them that the rally winner was eighty-seven years old. The amazing Gerry Crown, together with his brilliant co-driver Matt Bryson, an Australian rally champion, has won three out of the past four Paris Pekings. It goes without saying that they know what they are doing. Both were surprisingly approachable and would normally happily answer questions to assist those of us with much less skill (i.e. all of the rest of us). Their car is a model that will be unknown to most in Europe since it was only ever sold in Australia. It is a Leyland P76, which the late British Leyland introduced in Australia to compete against the Holdens and the Fords. Being engineered for Australia it was a tough car and surprisingly many survive despite a very small cohort of initial sales and lack of spare parts. It was introduced as British Leyland were failing in the 1970s and fell foul of high oil prices and was only sold for a few years. It was the only car (as opposed to lorry or bus) sold under the Leyland brand in the modern era and, despite getting some car of the year awards in Australia, it is remembered as a massive commercial failure.

Boris Gruzman and his son Eliot were strong contenders for the award for the drivers of the most inappropriate car. Jaguar E-types are wonderful cars but notoriously fragile. Boris and Eliot probably had more to do than any other participants on the rally to keep their car going. But they proved much more rugged than their car and every time it broke managed to put it back together again. It was a real credit to their grit and determination that they made it to the end.

Even less appropriate was the Ferrari. No one has ever taken a Ferrari on an endurance rally of this (or indeed any other) kind before and Giorgio Schön and Enrico Guggiari succeeded. They missed most of the Gobi Desert because Giorgio developed an illness that required him to be hospitalised. But he managed to discharge himself on the last day before they would have been disqualified. Enrico is an affable man who like me has ridden the Cresta Run in St Moritz (though my impression is that he took it rather more seriously than my amateur attempts!) so we have some friends in common. The Ferrari made it to the end, though it was delayed by being filled up with diesel and having to be cleaned out. I buy Shell V-Power diesel in the UK for one of my Jaguars, but I guess Shell must only sell V-Power petrol and not V-Power diesel in Italy which may explain the mistake of filling a Ferrari with diesel. Shell V-Power is the petrol of choice for many classic car owners because of its high octane rating.

Besides the super exotic were a wide range of Volvos, Datsun 240Zs, Porsches and Mercedes. One smart option was a Lada – if you think about it, by far the best choice for going across Russia, since every village blacksmith and most farmers in Russia can mend a Lada. There were a few Alfas, one of which (driven by Matteo and Roberto Crippa) we nicknamed the submarine because the driver managed to get it completely submerged on a river crossing. But it got dried out and continued the rally, epitomising the grit that was shown by so many participants. We were especially pleased that they made it back on the rally because they were charming company. Another Alfa was also driven by a very friendly pair of drivers, Gerard and Lorenzo Bas. They run a transport company and not surprisingly are unenthusiastic about the problems imposed on them by Brexit. It is to their credit that they were prepared to continue to discuss politics with me when my views on this subject are somewhat different from theirs.

On the first full day in Mongolia there was very nearly a fatality. A Porsche was totalled after being rolled six times. A loose part flew past and virtually took the ear off the navigator, who also broke his arm quite badly. He required multiple stitches and looked a real mess when we saw him the next day in the hotel. An inch the other way and it would have been a different level of seriousness. They were medivaced back to Europe. But believe it or not, even they reappeared a fortnight later in Russia. They had gone back to Europe, spent a few days in hospital, had the ear sewn back on, plastered the arm, bought another Porsche and driven back to finish the rest of the rally with us. Obviously with a new car they could not be classified. I suspect the phrase 'glutton for punishment' would not be misplaced here. But they deserved an award for their persistence…

Before the rally there is a weekend briefing section in Gaydon. On the middle evening when we were just about to go out for a curry we saw someone, clearly a participant, who looked at a loose end near the reception of our hotel. We immediately invited him to join us (a non-trivial task fitting a third person into the back of a Jaguar XJS sports car) and picked his brains about the rally. John Young is a canny Australian lawyer who had participated in a previous rally as a navigator. He and his partner Kerry Finn had hand prepared a Peugeot

504 beautifully. John's advice was very helpful – prepare your car well, be careful about weight, eat carefully. Apparently on most previous rallies people had been beset with tummy bugs – not nice when there are about five loos in the camping area for 250 people. One of the things that worked really well on this year's rally was that there were no widespread tummy bugs, and as a result the medical team were relatively underworked. They ended up mainly doing time checks for the rally and eventually creating their own business by running over someone's foot on the day after the sweeps' party.

We really felt for John and Kerry that they had the most awful luck with tyre blowouts. On the rally they managed to blow twenty-seven tyres, which may be a new record. But they still got to the end and put a very brave face on what must have been a disappointing trip.

Erik Andersen and Mary-Anne Elkington drove a 1950 metallic crimson Oldsmobile 88 Coupe. It was a beautiful car and expertly prepared. Their biggest problem was constantly getting stopped by traffic police which slightly worried Erik, who is a senior lawyer running the offices of Dentons in Papua New Guinea. I greatly enjoyed introducing him at our post-event lunch for our friends to my university friend Doran Doeh, who for many years ran the Dentons office in Moscow. Mary-Anne is a world-class athlete who was probably the only person ever to bring a bike, which she used frequently, on the Peking to Paris. They both tried to get us ballet tickets in St Petersburg but even Dentons' pull proved inadequate.

Andrew Barnes and Charlotte Lockhart picked up a Chevrolet 'Fangio' Coupe from Rally Preparation Services. They were a fun couple who seemed to suffer from the fact that the event organisers were leaning quite aggressively towards the event being a World Rally Championship type event rather than an endurance event for amateurs, which is what we as well as Andrew and Charlotte had certainly believed it to be. This conflict is one which the rally organisers will have to resolve at some point.

Andrew and Charlotte amongst other things run a winery on Waiheke Island in Auckland Bay. Ianthe and I had visited Waiheke when we were in New Zealand for the 2011 Rugby World Cup but chose to have lunch at a rather better-known winery before returning to Auckland to see England just beat Scotland at Eden Park, Auckland's iconic rugby venue. Andrew and Charlotte are also proselytisers for people working a four-day rather than a five-day week, though they agree that part of the deal is that people should raise their hourly productivity to achieve as much in four days as they would otherwise achieve in five days. Mike and I had a great Michelin-starred meal in Liège a few nights before the end of the rally with them both.

Probably the most exotic individuals on the rally were Jo and Heather Worth from Auckland (though Heather now works in Australia), who were on their second rally. Jo is a lively tomboyish lady who takes no prisoners when driving. Heather, her mother, is in her later years and must be extremely brave to accompany Jo. She is an academic sociologist who mainly studies the behaviour of sex workers in the Pacific Islands and elsewhere. We noticed that she applied her academic thoroughness to the process of navigation and we often followed her when we were uncertain about the route. They drove a much-battered Volvo Amazon that Jo had managed to smash up on the first day (nearly putting her out of the rally).

Philip and Trish Monks drove a Mark II 3.4 Jaguar which looked good despite the lengths of duct tape necessary to stop the rear window from escaping when the body flexed. As my father had once had a Mark II I had some sympathy, though we often found ourselves behind them trying to overtake.

Amongst the more beautiful cars on the rally was the Jensen Interceptor of Serge and Jacqui Berthier. They didn't have much luck on the rally and spent nights in some exotic places but we had an entertaining evening with them at the Belgian party in Liège when they finally caught up.

Barry Nash and Malcolm Lister drove a heavily modified Rover P5B which just kept on going. Barry runs a rally preparation garage in Benenden near where both Mike and I live in Tenterden and when driving past I occasionally stop to have a quick chat. Their car was as well prepared as anyone's and according to the sweeps it probably required less maintenance than any other car on the rally.

Another well-prepared car was Jamie Turner's and Julian Riley's Morris Minor. Their car was not exactly standard but a very good example of how to make a rally car from a vehicle that in its own time was not exactly known for reliability. It was also beautifully turned out. Though when I let Julian ahead of me in a queue for coffee he said, 'You'll never make a rallier if you do things like that'.

Also with a smaller-engined car that competed successfully were John and Chris Beresford in a Volkswagen. They were driving a 1956 car that had been bought for John's wife Deirdre, who had died after a long debilitating battle with rheumatoid arthritis three years ago. They restored her car and converted it into a rally car to raise money for the Arthritis Society. They were the only Canadian team in the rally.

Steve Partridge and Corgi La Grouw competed in an old Morris Oxford from the 1950s of the kind that was reissued as a Hindustan in India. This car was in its second Peking to Paris and seemed to keep on running. It also managed pretty decent times on the quicker stages.

Michael Eatough and his son Marcus drove a Mercedes 230S 'Fintail'. When these cars were made they were amongst the toughest cars around and there were a number of Fintails on the rally. Michael, who works in the motor trade as his day job, had prepared his car well and seemed to have few problems that were apparent from the outside. He also had an endless supply of entertaining stories to keep the rest of us amused.

Joseph Lemmens from the Netherlands is a property developer with interests in art galleries. He drove a Mercedes SLC with his son Patrick. His views on property seem quite similar to mine and I was delighted to introduce him to Stewart Labrooy, one of my oldest friends, who is Malaysia's leading property investor.

Enrico Paggi and Frederica Mascetti drove a beautiful Fiat 124 Spyder. They had clearly thought through how to handle the people who might crowd around them – they had printed child-sized T-shirts which they handed out to small children. Frederica has a way with the bambini and children and they besieged her everywhere she went. We were envious of her talent though I was very grateful that Mike had had the presence of mind to print out cards with pictures of our car and its make and year to give to people.

Renee Brinkerhoff is rallying around the world in her Porsche 356 with a film crew in tow. Her co-driver, the wonderfully presidentially named Calvin Cooledge, is an experienced rally expert. Renee was always good fun and although her car didn't always match her ambition, she remained cheerful. In St Petersburg, the guru of Porsche engineers, Francis Tuthill, flew in and replaced her entire engine. That can't have been cheap... Calvin was also entertaining company with a fund of stories and would normally join us for a glass of something.

Lars and Annette Rolner drove a heavily converted Porsche 911 that had clearly been the recipient of much investment. He apparently has fifteen other Porsches and, given his generosity with Havana cigars, is probably not short of a bob or two. But he mucked in with the rest of us and (except when his cigars got dangerously close to our often leaking fuel lines) was always intriguing to be with.

I've always been a sucker for older British sports cars. Ianthe and I met when my Triumph TR6 broke down on my way to the wedding of one of my flatmates. And so it was not surprising that one of my favourite rally cars was 'Gidget', an Austin Healey driven by Ashton Roskill and navigated by Giles Cooper. On the writing on the side of the car where participants listed their names they had run out of space and so had shortened 'Driver Ashton Roskill' to 'Dr Ashton Roskill', so he became known on the rally as 'the doctor'. We had met and enjoyed the company of Giles at the Gaydon event and spent some good times with him and Ashton in the rally evenings. We managed to help them out one morning leaving Ufa when their electrics had failed. Mike's tool chest managed to find a device which enabled them to isolate the problem.

All of us on the rally had fellow feelings for the other participants who were facing the same problems and obstacles. But the closest thing to a divide on the rally was between those who were definitely competing for prizes or classification and those like us whose objective was simply to get to the end. Some of those who were competing took the competition to great lengths – occasionally a plane would appear and out of it a team of mechanics, often equipped with an engine or a gearbox, or a similarly equipped truck would suddenly come over the horizon. Some spent millions. Others tried what they could with what they could carry with them. But we all faced essentially the same challenge – it's just that we coped in different ways.

We made some great friends on the rally and have kept in touch with many of them since, through social media and email. Friendships forged in the stress of the rally have a resilience to them which helps them last.

6

DAY MINUS 5 TO DAY ZERO: STARTING IN BEIJING

DAY MINUS 5

We are in Beijing for the start of the rally. Although it is not the largest city in the world (Tokyo) or even the largest in China (Chongqing and Shanghai are larger) it is still twice the size of London, with a population of 21 million. And yet it seemed today curiously empty, although the roads were uniformly jammed.

Our luxurious hotel, chosen as the best place to park more than a hundred classic cars, was near the 2nd Ring Road and also near to the rather lovely Purple Bamboo Park where we managed to get lost in the evening (but what a place in which to get lost!)

Beijing seems in many ways to be the centre of the world – the clear capital and leading city in what is already the world's second largest economy and which will soon be the largest. In the last ten years China has accounted for 40 per cent of the world's economic growth and you can see the proof of this in the rising living standards in Beijing, which now seem to have reached roughly the level where Singapore was about twenty years ago.

The morning started with Mike and I press releasing Cebr's Belt and Road study in the hotel lobby. We coincided with a property conference. As the Chinese buy property with suit-cases of cash the security was impressive. Fortunately we had briefed *China Daily* in advance and there was a good report in their international edition.[34]

Our report shows that the Belt and Road Initiative will transform the world economy, particularly Central Asia and Russia. But our guess is that Western Europe will join in, with Holland (surely Rotterdam is the western end?) and the UK also benefitting. The country most affected proportionately is predicted to be Mongolia, through which we will be driving in a week's time. So we will be able to see for ourselves!

Having disposed of work we went off to visit the Bell Tower and the Drum Tower.

The Bell Tower was closed for renovation. But we climbed the steep staircase in the Drum Tower to read about the ancient Chinese seasons, where voles turn into quails (Qingming) and where pheasants turn into clams (Lidong). The drums are huge and it must have been terrifying for the population to hear them, which normally meant an army was approaching. The nearest recent equivalent in the West must have been air raid sirens.

Then we visited various hutongs and had a drink by the lake before finding a Malaysian restaurant nearby which we had last visited in 2012. The owner also came from Petaling Jaya like Mike and me, which was a coincidence. The food was exceptional – curry ayam, rendang and satay – by far the best Malaysian I have had except in Kuala Lumpur. Mike and I enjoyed nattering in our broken Malay with John Paul Cho, the owner.

The hotel is starting to fill up with rally crews. They all seem frighteningly knowledgeable. We had a quick drink with one lady who is taking her eighty-year-old mother as navigator (not sure I would have done that to my mother, even when she was only eighty!) and an American gentleman who when we asked if he knew about cars turned out to be the top adviser on classic cars to Bonhams... bit of a faux pas that one!

Then a quick (as we had thought) walk to the local supermarket to buy provisions. Alas, Apple Maps turned out to be out of date – no supermarket at all but instead a lovely patch of green with lakes and islands, Beijing's Purple Bamboo Park. Sadly my phone had discharged, so we ended up walking about five miles instead of the one mile intended because the maps application was no longer available and we turned the wrong way more than once. But it really was pleasant. The park is filled with more than fifty varieties of bamboo and a third of its area is lake, with spectacular lotus blossoms and water lilies. We really didn't mind getting lost even if our feet complained a bit as we got back to the hotel. We had an early night because Rowena and Mike have booked a tour of the Forbidden City and Summer Palace and the guide was due to fetch us at 8 a.m.

DAY MINUS 4

I have a reputation in my family for being the last to arrive or to get up and for keeping everyone else waiting, so I was quite amused that when Ianthe phoned Mike and Rowena this morning they were still asleep. They did well to appear fully clothed and looking smart within fifteen minutes.

Our excellent and feisty tour guide Joyce[35] was waiting with a people carrier to take us to the Forbidden City through Beijing's morning rush hour. The pace was about the same as the Marylebone Road at an equivalent time of day.

We were kept waiting by a motorcade – there appears to be a state visit happening, though we did not recognise the flag (it turns out to be the African state of Niger). The highlight of the procession for petrolheads was two Hongqi L5s. These are huge cars that Westerners hardly ever see since they are reserved for the use of the very top leaders in China (and presumably their official guests).[36]

The central public areas of Beijing were being spruced up for 1 October 2019, when the seventieth anniversary of the revolution is being celebrated. And one sensed that the country was building up for this. The local TV was full of programmes highlighting the achievements of the regime.

The Forbidden City has only been open to the public since the 1920s and consists of over 600 imperial buildings.

It was clearly designed to impress and succeeds. The number of visitors is huge, as the queues indicate. But the place is also huge. We walked about four miles from the southern entrance in Tiananmen Square to the Imperial Gardens at the northern end of the Forbidden City.

When the Forbidden City was built during the fifteenth century, China's GDP was about one and a half times that of all of Western Europe, and China's annual GDP per capita was about $600 (in 1990 Geary–Khamis dollars).[37] To put this in perspective, at the time of the revolution in 1949 China's GDP per capita on the same measure had fallen to $450. On this measure Chinese GDP per capita is roughly $15,000 today. One can see why the regime is so keen to emphasise how far the country has travelled since the revolution – they now have a fairly impressive story to tell in economic terms, though forty years ago, before they changed their economic policy, the story looked less good.

Walking round the streets in Beijing, there are many fewer people who look obviously poor than one might expect in a country that until recently had a relatively low level of national income per capita. And it does appear that the Chinese government has been hugely successful in its objective of reducing poverty. The United Nations' Sustainable Development Goal number 1 is the reduction in poverty worldwide. There has been substantial success here since the goal was first established in 1990 and 70 per cent of the reduction of the numbers in poverty over this period has been in China.*

Interestingly, the Chinese government, as part of its plan to improve the quality of growth, is increasingly focusing on poverty reduction in rural areas and in less developed regions such as Western China. Their strategy has three elements: increase human capital through investments in health and education; improve infrastructure, particularly road and rail; and finally direct encouragement of economic development with strategies to increase tourism in the rural areas and attempts to develop the poorer regions of the country, partly through the Belt and Road Initiative.

In 1860 the Brits and French (oddly on the same side) burned Beijing's Summer Palace. When I explained this to fellow rally participants from the US over breakfast they pointed out that the Brits also burned the White House during the nineteenth century and the replastering and painting in white after this was what gave the building its modern name! So the nineteenth-century Brits seemed to like burning palaces!

---

* For a much more detailed discussion of this see my recently published book *The Inequality Paradox*, Abrams, 2019. The paradox is that poverty has fallen as inequality has risen.

DAY MINUS 3

I missed the trip to the (rebuilt) Summer Palace yesterday afternoon but Ianthe, Rowena and Mike had a leisurely visit, walking around lakes and admiring the architecture. I rested with a slightly stretched back, not wanting to risk further damage before the rally, and had a chance to read the local press and see some TV.

I get the impression that China is quite nervous at the moment. They clearly are worried by President Trump and the trade war. The local press is full of articles explaining why China can withstand the trade war, which suggests a degree of worry about whether this is really the case. There is also a degree of nervousness about the fact that growth appears to have slowed sharply last year, by much more than is admitted in the official figures.* Although there are some signs of a recovery and there has been a massive fiscal and monetary stimulus, there are still doubts about how far this recovery will take hold.

Tomorrow will be another leisurely day while the others visit the Great Wall. So watch out for more reflections on the state of the Chinese economy!

---

* At least, this is a commonly shared view amongst China-watching experts. The main reason we think this is the evidence from economic data about China that comes from sources outside China like data on exports to China. In theory the trade data might be affected by third factors breaking the link between trade and growth but in practice, imports of essential products, which are not affected by trade restrictions, normally give a pretty good guide to the pace of the economy.

I got a mini kicking from one of my colleagues a fortnight ago for making observations about the Spanish economy based mainly on what I had seen. But my confidence in my ability to make sound economic observations was revived when my rough guess that Beijing's GDP per capita was about the same as Singapore's had been twenty years ago seemed to be backed up by the numbers once I had bothered to do the calculations to test my intuition.

China's purchasing power parity GDP per capita is currently about $17,000 (Cebr estimate) compared with about $50,000 for Singapore twenty years ago. But there is huge regional income inequality in China, as a recent study from the St Louis Fed suggests.

The St Louis Fed analysis shows that household incomes in Beijing are about 2.2 times the Chinese average,[38] so using the ratio of household incomes to scale up GDP, it suggests that for the whole of Beijing GDP per capita is $37,000. OK, not quite $50,000 but in the same ballpark and, bearing in mind that I am currently only looking at central Beijing, and incomes in the centres of major metropolises are normally higher than the average, probably a pretty good observation.

Ianthe asked me how I could possibly judge GDP per capita simply by looking around a bit. And actually I was stumped when she asked because it has become instinctive. So I am trying to work out my process for judging the prosperity of an economy. This is my attempt to explain (to myself as much as to anyone else)...

The first thing I look at is people in menial jobs. In really poor countries these people's bodies are emaciated to the point where I can hardly bear to look at them, damaged by years of malnutrition. If people doing jobs like hotel cleaner, road sweeper, watchman and so on are looking well fed and clearly have been for a while, it is likely that the economy is doing reasonably well. Labour markets at the bottom end in emerging economies are fairly competitive and if people doing relatively unskilled jobs earn enough to eat well, it suggests that they have moved some way up the income scale. It is unlikely that the people doing the jobs that I notice will be paid very differently from those doing similarly skilled jobs elsewhere in the same travel to work area. Employers will not deliberately overpay their labour force. On that basis China left the bottom rung of the ladder about a quarter of a century ago.

Next I look at clothing, again focusing most on the poorest people. If they are wearing rags it tells one story. If they have newish clean clothes, it tells another, since they must have a number of changes of clothes for any set to be clean. Clothing comes after food in most countries (though not all). Again China has clearly climbed up past the stage of dirty ragged clothing and has even largely passed the polyester stage.

If people doing menial jobs are doing reasonably well, it is likely that those in better jobs are doing better, and it becomes possible to make some kind of a guess as to how well the whole economy is doing.

Then I look at the shops. If the shops are filled up with stock, this suggests that there is a vibrant consumer economy. The biggest cost to retailers is inventory, so they can only afford to fill shelves if items are moving quickly. Beijing shops are not that different from those in the West, but remind me more of those in Singapore in the 1990s, which was the main basis of my observation about GDP.

Then I look at the types of things that people are buying. There is a whole hierarchy of purchases as people move from poor to rich. These days the next purchases after food and clothes tend to be consumer electronics. So it is interesting to see how widespread these are. And other consumer items and what sort of luxuries can be afforded on a widespread basis.

As someone who knows cars reasonably well, I obviously look closely at what cars, bikes, motorbikes and scooters are on the road, and how new they are. Mike observed on Sunday how much newer the cars on Beijing roads are now than those he had seen when he was last in Beijing four years ago.

China holds the world record for the longest ever traffic jam of twelve days (as I cheerfully reminded Ianthe, Rowena and Mike when we were stuck in a jam coming from the airport on Sunday), suggesting that people are owning cars to a greater extent than the authorities had predicted...[39]

Next I look at the public infrastructure: its quality, its newness and upkeep – particularly the latter. Though sometimes in dictatorship the infrastructure is looked after better than the level of economic performance would suggest, there is normally some kind of relationship between infrastructure and prosperity.

Finally I normally look at property prices and quality. There are two elements to property prices, supply and demand, and one needs to understand both. The US is much richer than the UK, yet UK property prices are mainly higher, partly because of supply-side factors like lack of land and planning.

The average selling price for second-hand homes in Beijing in February 2019 was 59,898 yuan (US $8,920) per square metre, down 11.3 per cent from the level seen in March 2017.[40] Beijing prices are about the same as in Amsterdam but twice those in Kuala Lumpur.

Because of the way Chinese money is invested in property, which distorts prices,* on this occasion I have ignored Beijing property prices as a guide to standards of living.

---

* There is a tendency in China (as indeed elsewhere in the East but to a more pronounced extent) to understate profits. The undeclared profits are conventionally turned into cash and then invested in the property market in the names of nominee companies. This means that the money cannot easily be traced. But one of the consequences is that property prices in China are typically higher than would normally be the case for a country with equivalent economic fundamentals.

I have the good fortune to be able to remember what Malaysia and Singapore were like as their incomes grew from $3–4,000 in modern PPP GDP per capita terms in the 1950s to Singapore's current level of $86,000. What is interesting is that the rules I use seem to work well while a country is moving from $3,000 PPP GDP to about $30,000. It is much harder to see the difference between $30,000 and $80,000 using these techniques! But my experience from the Far East gives me a pretty good base to calibrate movements of GDP per capita as countries move up the lower reaches of the income scale.

All this tells me that China (or at least Beijing) is still doing well, though there are hints of difficulties on the horizon, as the falling property prices suggest.

Ianthe has just come back from the Great Wall. Terrible traffic jams on the 3rd Ring Road to get there but she, Rowena and Mike really enjoyed having a chance to walk on this amazing monument. They also tobogganed down which they appear to have enjoyed, providing photographic evidence!

They saw the Bird's Nest on the way out, which they had really wanted to see. So they seem to have had a good day. I've been resting my back, which is feeling much better.

Rally fever is building up in the hotel. More and more people are joining in and all seem very friendly. Tomorrow we will receive a stern lecture on driving in China from the Beijing chief of police. Obviously we will all behave ourselves!

DAY MINUS 2

We had a leisurely breakfast today before chasing after our chores. First task was to buy food supplies for the rally in case we missed any stops or got hungry during the day. Lots of bottled water (not worth having fizzy on a trip that is likely to be bouncy!) and dried food.

Then back to the hotel in time for the lecture on Chinese road safety by the local chief of traffic police presided over by the chief of police. Impressive set of three senior police plus an interpreter, all impeccably turned out and looking thoroughly competent. Fairly basic lecture but still quite useful reminders of the differences between driving in China and the rest of the world. Although warning us that we have to look out for cyclists, a category of road user with whom Westerners might not be familiar, suggested they hadn't visited Islington or Camden recently!

The lecture was a requirement for us to be issued temporary Chinese driving licences which happens on Friday before we are allowed to collect our cars.

The rest of the afternoon and evening was spent in the company of Patrick Debussere and Bernard Vereenooghe, who needed a new battery, while we searched the car suppliers of the city for octane enhancer. We don't need it in China (at least Beijing) where 92- and 95-octane petrol and even the wonderful Shell V-Power are easily available. But in parts of

Mongolia and Russia we are uncertain so we figured it was best to be prepared.

There is an area in Beijing where there is a mall consisting entirely of people selling things for cars, with body shops and repair shops on the ground floor. Sam, the interpreter for the rally team, kindly took Patrick, Bernard, Mike and me to this 'car city' to hunt for our needed supplies. Because octane enhancer is unnecessary in Beijing, the first forty shops we tried had none. But just as we were about to leave Sam found some. We have invested heavily in the product! Patrick and Bernard have a beautiful 1933 Dodge convertible.

We got back quite late and decided to test out the restaurant across the road from the hotel that had been highly recommended by not only other ralliers but also even the staff from the hotel. Despite minor communication issues, we had our best meal so far. It also happened to be the cheapest, the meal for four costing about the same as my lunch for one in the hotel the previous day. The Beijing duck was a revelation.

We came back to the hotel full and happy. Tomorrow we collect the cars and things start to get exciting! The buzz of anticipation is getting even stronger as everyone starts to focus on the rally.

DAY MINUS 1

Signing on was at 9 a.m., at which point we were told when we should collect our cars. Mike and I got allocated to the second bus which left at 10 a.m.

We were delighted to discover the car had arrived at the warehouse. Less so that the transport company had drained out all the fuel from many of the cars, and even less so when they claimed that the problem had been 'evaporation', an excuse that was hardly likely to wash with someone like Mike, with a first class honours degree in engineering, or even me, with rather less scientific knowledge. We had to wait for two hours while replacement fuel arrived.

Eventually we got the fuel and took the car back to the hotel. The engine was running rather lumpily and Mike had to utilise his skills of diagnosis and mechanics.

He cleaned the spark plugs, dismantled one of the carburettors and rebuilt and adjusted the choke mechanism. What probably would solve the problem would be a blast at reasonable speed down a motorway, which hopefully we will do tomorrow.

Then the party and dinner. Most of which passed in a blur.

DAY ZERO

Saturday was reserved for scrutineering and putting on stickers. Rowena and Ianthe worked marvels to put stickers of a range of kinds on the car and smooth them down. Putting stickers on cars is actually a pretty complicated task and I was grateful to Rowena and Ianthe for their doing it for us, and also to Rowena for planning where they went.

We are also particularly grateful to those who provided them: Cebr, of course, Inverlochy Castle, Fair Fuel, Nicholson Gin and Stellar Fuel Additives. Much appreciated. We also have a sticker for the Harinder Veriah Trust, for whom we are fundraising.

Mike took the car to scrutineering, where he used his persuasive skills to deal with a variety of problems, the most difficult of which was a non-working horn. Horns are an essential part of automotive equipment in Asia so this was an issue we had to sort.

In between our getting the equipment into the car and sorting out stickers, Alexis Hooi of *China Daily* came to interview us. We had a lot in common since he was brought up in Singapore and Mike and I in Malaysia. He came with a cameraman and we interviewed on camera for him, Mike talking with great eloquence about the technical modifications made to the car.

Then a final briefing for competitors to tell us various slightly important things like the route for the following day and details for the official start of the rally at the Great Wall. And our start times.

I am finishing this off at 4 a.m. on Sunday morning Beijing time. Today we have the fancy start of the rally at the

Great Wall and drive to Hohhot, which is the capital of Inner Mongolia and the centre of a metropolitan area of over 3 million people. Wish us luck!

Meanwhile Alexis Hooi's article appeared in *China Daily* and then later in the *Daily Telegraph* in London. It said:

More than 200 motoring enthusiasts from across the globe went behind the wheels of their classic and vintage cars, including Bentleys, Porsches and Alfa Romeos, on Saturday in Beijing to gear up for an epic endurance drive from the Chinese capital to Paris.

The 36-day rally, considered one of the world's toughest motoring challenges, stretches about 13,000 km and covers more than 10 countries and regions through the Asian continent and on to Western Europe, including the harsh deserts of the Gobi and wide expanse of Siberia, according to event organizers.

The first 'Peking to Paris' motor rally was held in 1907 and took about two months. This is its seventh edition this year and retains one of its most striking characteristics – the participants will be driving only cars manufactured before the late 1970s as they follow in the tracks of the rally pioneers.

The vehicles are set to traverse gravel, sand and stunning mountain roads and plains, with motorists getting the chance to sleep in tents under the stars on the steppes of Mongolia.

There are altogether 106 two-person teams taking on the challenge, which entry fee alone cost about $70,000. The teams roll out from the Juyongguan section of the Great Wall early Sunday and are expected to drive into Paris on July 7 through the finish line at the Place Vendôme.

There will be support and logistics groups, but the participants are expected to carry out regular maintenance on their own cars and obviously, stock important spare parts since the rare cars are very different from each other. Average daily distances to be covered are about 400 km but can be as much as 650 km.

Briton Douglas McWilliams will be in his 1958 Bentley S1 model with his brother Mike McWilliams, a top-notch engineer who will lead the maintenance of their car as well as any repairs it needs on the journey. Modifications to their luxury car include strengthened suspension, a rebuilt gearbox and a new air filter for the engine.

'For us, the challenge is to take a car like this, a Bentley, across the Gobi Desert, a car that's more suited to maybe driving to the opera or going on a tour around London. So the car has been prepared quite specially for the rally. The route is very challenging, in Mongolia there are barely any roads at all,' Mike told China Daily at a gathering point for the motorists in the Shangri-La Hotel, Beijing.

Other than the obvious obstacles en route, Douglas, founder and deputy chairman of the London-based

Centre for Economics and Business Research consultancy, also considers the experience important because he will be able to see for himself the areas that will be covered by the China-proposed Belt and Road Initiative global infrastructure and development project.

Douglas said he will personally assess the potential of these areas when they are linked up by better transport networks and improved trade facilities. He is writing a book about the rally and the BRI called 'Driving the Silk Road'.

'Mike and I were brought up in Malaysia and it used to be a frequent topic of discussion amongst the expatriates, about going back to the UK overland. We've always been excited by the prospects of being able to do it,' he said.

Now, with the Belt and Road Initiative and China helping to develop infrastructure connecting the East and West, Douglas said he would be able to make comparisons between the old and new trade routes.

'I'm fascinated by the Belt and Road Initiative, I think it's the most important infrastructure initiative ever. Being able to contrast the old-fashioned way of travelling across land to Europe with the newfangled ways now being created, it's such a wonderful opportunity,' he said.

7

DAY 1 TO DAY 3: TO THE WESTERN EDGE OF CHINA

DAY 1

At last the great day has arrived and Mike and I left the hotel at 5.30 a.m., with Rowena and Ianthe getting the supporters' bus for the 7 a.m. start of the rally at the Great Wall.

They laid on an amazing party for us all with dragon dances, lion dancers, acrobats, drummers and the lot to send us off.

It was a real treat that Ianthe and Rowena came to see us off. We are both looking forward to seeing them again in Paris.

Our day has had three themes. Quite a lot of it has been spent in traffic jams. The route along the Wall is clearly a Sunday favourite and by the time we had been flagged off we were sent into the middle of a traffic jam that lasted about ninety minutes. Eventually it thinned out. As we passed a toll booth we passed a pickup truck with, amazingly, a couple of ponies standing in the back. They seemed perfectly happy, though the method of transport can hardly be called safe.

The second theme has been spectacular scenery. First we were taken through a beautiful valley that could have been in the Scottish Highlands in shape, though the colours were a little different. The road was a gravel track with only one lane so lots of backing up and edging past took place. Then in the afternoon we drove up some lovely hills that could have been in southern Spain.

The third theme has been the extraordinary speed of economic development in China. We arrived in Hohhot, the capital of Inner Mongolia, this evening. This is an amazing place. If you believe the figures its average annual rate of economic growth in the 2000s has been 24.8 per cent. Its GDP is 132 times what it was forty years ago. I counted sixty-one cranes as I passed and there are surely more. The population is already 3 million and still growing fast. It specialises in food products, energy and technology. About half the growth now comes from technology companies and it is a major centre for big data.

The pace of growth has led to a massive traffic jam as we arrived that delayed us for two hours and was only solved by someone opening the barrier so that we could drive down the wrong side of the road (oddly we discovered that the cars going down that side had been diverted to our carriageway). The jam must have lasted well into the night (though we passed close by the next morning and there were no signs of the previous night's traffic problems).

It is clear that if you drive to Western China you can see a very different pace of economic development from the calmer (although still rapid by Western standards) rate of growth in more familiar places like Beijing and Shanghai.

As the Belt and Road Initiative develops, this is the part of China which is likely to be transformed even more.

DAY 2

One of the advantages of having a relatively late starting position is that we have plenty of time for breakfast (but not always – see Erenhot!). So when we were told that our breakfast was in the restaurant on the twenty-sixth floor of our hotel we were pleased. And what a view – we chose the table with the best view and settled down to enjoy our view over the mountains. (Besides being one of the world's most extraordinary cities economically – like Petaling Jaya, where we were brought up, but much bigger and growing as if on steroids – Hohhot is also tucked in beside mountains high enough to be ski resorts in the winter.)

But by the time we had queued for the one espresso machine serving 300 Westerners used to getting their breakfast coffee fix the view seemed to have changed to one of expressways under construction. Gradually we caught on that we were in fact having breakfast in a restaurant that revolved!

We didn't have a great start to the day and my navigating was entirely to blame. I missed a right turn immediately after the hotel and we drove around in a circle twice before Mike pointed out my mistake. He was not entirely pleased.

We arrived at the dirt track for the first speed trial an hour late but for some reason didn't get penalised as we deserved to be. Since the previous day we had been penalised for being caught in a traffic jam, which was more the fault of the organisers than ours, so I guess these things even out.

The speed trial was great fun even in a two-ton Bentley, which is not really the car you would choose for such an event. We raced round a track of about a mile on a dirt road and made lots of dust. Mike drove conservatively but even so made good progress.

Then we drove through what must be the mainstay of the Inner Mongolian tourist industry. First we drove up to what appeared to be one of their ski resorts (the temperature in Hohhot, belying its name, falls to an average of –10 degrees Celsius in the winter), looking rather parched and dry in the summer, and then through the great grasslands, which resemble what much of the Midwest of the US must have looked like before being cultivated.

The fact that China has ski resorts is a reminder that Beijing is the site of the 2022 Winter Olympics, with some of the events due to take place quite close to the Great Wall where the rally started.

There seemed to be plenty of yurt camps in the prairies, where people spend a few days living in yurts (called *gers* locally) and riding Mongolian horses. Though business didn't seem all that good – most seemed empty of customers.

The drive into Erenhot was on a fast straight road and I made pretty decent progress. We will discover when we get to the border whether the automatic number recognition system has built up a series of speeding fines (or worse...). But by the time we arrived we had caught up the lost hour!

One of the noticeable themes of China is that when they decide to do something they do it big. We passed a field of solar panels at least a kilometre in length before seeing field after field of propellers.

It turned out that we had reached the biggest wind farm in the world. This, the Ulanqab Wind Power Base, is still in the course of completion and is eventually planned to produce 6 gigawatts of energy from a field (or more precisely a series of fields) covering 3,800 square kilometres! The propellers stretch way beyond the horizon. Technically this isn't a Belt and Road project. But it showed the sort of project that might well be replicated.

Erenhot is the border town, population 80,000, on the Chinese side of the border between China and Mongolia. It received an economic boost when the railway axle change operation, necessary because of the different gauges in China and Mongolia, was transferred there in the 1960s. But it is also famous for its dinosaurs. Dinosaur fossils have been found near Erenhot since the mid-1990s and the authorities have capitalised on this to build theme parks and statues. You can't miss them.

The rally must be one of the biggest things to hit Erenhot and the locals put on a show for us, with their local version of Beyoncé singing her heart out. Sadly loud pop music wasn't what we really wanted after a hard day's driving and we gave her precious little support.

When you are staying in a rather dubious-looking hotel one of the tricks (so I'm told) is not to pay any attention to the knocks on the door offering things. So when we heard a knock on the door at 10 p.m. my instinct was to ignore it. But Mike decided to open it, and fortunately so.

A disgruntled Nick, one of the organisers, had clearly drawn the short straw, which was to go round every participant's hotel room and warn us that because of likely blockages at the China–Mongolia border, our start time had been brought forward. Ours had moved from 9.37 a.m. to 7 a.m. and breakfast was at 6!

So much for our lie-in... we adjusted the alarm time and (fortunately) went to sleep.

DAY 3

Though our start time had been brought forward to 7 a.m., when we appeared at that time most people had left. So we drove as fast as we decently could to the border. We had been warned of a convoy of heavy lorries that we had to beat to the border to get in front of them in the queue. We arrived at the border to find a long queue of rally cars only. The border was still shut, despite rumours that someone had been 'incentivised' to open it early.

Exiting China was relatively easy. There were queues but people and cars were processed efficiently and about an hour after the border was opened we had all got through. We thought the hard work was done.

Little did we know of the difficulties of getting into Mongolia.

Even queuing is a non-trivial task. Queue jumping is clearly the Mongolian national sport and with their weapon of choice being Russian World War 2 ex-army jeeps they had, as they say in the boxing ring, a height and weight advantage. We fought our place valiantly but even we had to give way to seven or eight vehicles. One particularly aggressive queue jumper got a dose of his own medicine when a rally car driver reversed into him. The rally car had clearly strengthened its rear end and this version of 'Paris parking' left a hole in the Mongolian vehicle. Though you can understand the frustration of people used to getting through customs and immigration quickly every day suddenly discovering that they have to wait three hours while an entire rally from abroad is let through.

We joined the queue at 9.30 and finally got through at about 12.30. By then the rally schedule was a mess, further hampered by a lake that was meant to be dry having flooded last week.

There was a proper road at the border but it lasted a few hundred metres before disappearing, with an eighteen-inch drop to the new base. Then about 10 kilometres looking out for orange flags put out by ERA, the rally organisers, leading us on dirt tracks to the next proper road. Which lasted 220 kilometres to the desert. The last town before the desert was a real frontier town, with twelve petrol stations and lots of recent development.

Then we started the rally proper.

8

DAY 3 TO DAY 8: CROSSING THE GOBI DESERT

STILL DAY 3

Driving in the desert is a real thrill. It's a complicated calculation getting the right balance between concern for the longevity of your car and the need to make progress. I was probably too protective of the car (partly because I owned it and would have to pay for any damage done!). Mike, with many years of experience driving on unmade-up roads in Zambia, Botswana, Sabah and other emerging economies, seemed (at the time) to get it right. Though time will tell...

Navigation is an art. We worked out that there were various inconsistencies between the route book and what was preloaded on the GPS. The latter turned out to be of more use.

Eventually we found a sea of wigwams like a vision out of a cowboy film – though the Wild West image was spoiled by the petrol tankers with three jerrycans of 20 litres each for each car. And latrines. And a beer tent. And a restaurant. And mechanics with welding equipment. And even an engine hoist. But the guards were on horseback to complete the Wild West image...

Nomads, who have set up the camp, are clearly a very professional organisation. Their kit, like so much in Mongolia, looks to have been bought from the Soviet military as Cold War surplus.

And none the worse for that. Equipment tends to be over-engineered and most items are bigger and stronger than they need to be. But that's quite reassuring in the middle of a desert.

Mike has investigated camping in a serious way. And put together really high-tech equipment that is the envy of everyone else. A three-room tent with separate bedrooms! An air mattress. Fabulous duck-feather-lined sleeping bags. Silk liners. Hanging torches to provide interior lighting. He even thoughtfully provided me with a second pillow. It was much more luxurious than our Erenhot hotel the previous night. And no knocks in the middle of the night to tell us our start time has been advanced! Our Italian friends said: 'not a tent, an apartment'.

We have the relatively gentle start time of 11.13, so plenty of time to work on the car in the morning.

One parting thought. As we departed China, the immigration people came out to take pics. One charming lady who spoke a little English asked where we came from. When we said London she said, 'I dream that one day I can visit London.' Those of us who are a bit blasé about living there should just remember that for some, just a few days in London would be a dream come true. I hope that it does for her...

DAY 4

There is nothing quite like rally driving in a classic car in the desert.

It imposes three challenges. First, the car is constantly being beaten by bouncing up and down on uneven ground. Gradually this takes a toll. The driver has to choose between maintaining an even pace and putting too much strain on the car, all the time trying to avoid the worst of the potholes, while the navigator has to use intuition to decide which of several trails all going in different directions to choose. Sometimes the intuition is wrong...

We started day four of the rally in our campsite. Breakfast was perhaps a bit too leisurely and by the time we had completed all our preparations and dismantled the amazing tent we managed to get a small penalty for starting a minute late. In the scheme of things a pretty minor problem and we both laughed it off.

Our cars had been filled from jerrycans at the camp – the organisers brought in a petrol lorry. The system worked pretty well and we got refuelled not long after we arrived.

Before we got going, Mike spent quite a while fixing various issues with the car. The sticking carburettor or whatever is causing the engine not to run properly was inspected and he cleaned the plugs (yet again!), an exhaust manifold had loosened and he tightened the bolts, and he wired up the rear of the exhaust where the mounting had broken. Meanwhile he also helped some of the other crews – by the time we got going he had lent tools or equipment to about five of the other competitors.

The organisers had set us a tough route today, made tougher by small inconsistencies between the route book (the bible that tells us what to do) and the GPS instructions. Combined with a late start, an impossibly fast schedule, our stopping to help broken-down cars and horrendous traffic jams on the way into Ulaanbaatar, we arrived at our hotel at nearly 10 p.m.

Driving across the desert makes a strong case for the various infrastructures that are planned in China's Belt and Road Initiative. Indeed, Cebr's report on the subject says that proportionately Mongolia will benefit more than any other country from the provision of decent infrastructure.[41]

Mongolia is very short of infrastructure. According to Cebr's World Economic League Table (WELT) for 2019:[42]

Vast reserves of mineral deposits and the foreign direct investment that these attracted were what underpinned Mongolia's transition from an agriculture based economy to one based on the extraction and export of commodities.

Mongolia's exports – two thirds of which are destined for China – account for 60 per cent of GDP. Copper ore, gold, coal, oil, iron and zinc ore are[43] among the country's major exports. Mongolia's dependence on mineral exports – in particular to China – means that the economy is highly exposed to both commodity price swings and demand from China. Rising commodity prices and a rapidly expanding Chinese economy hungry for commodities

fuelled rapid GDP growth for Mongolia after the turn of
the millennium.

The problem is that the minerals require transport to reach
their users. And good transport links are one of the many
things that Mongolia lacks.

Today's route was as tough on cars as on the participants
and we frequently had to stop to help others. Mike is fast
emerging as one of the characters of the rally with his intrepid
driving and his willingness to help out others in distress. It's
great but of course he gets rather more requests for help than
he can easily handle. One team today thought they had run
out of fuel and Mike got a mouthful of petrol as he syphoned
some from our tank – only to find that the team had actually
got an ignition problem!

We passed an enormous monument to Genghis Khan. The
not very politically correct custom in his day was that if you
conquered a country its women became your possessions. As a
result it is estimated that 0.5 per cent of today's world's population have Genghis Khan's genes!

Ulaanbaatar contains the bulk of Mongolia's otherwise
sparse population. The mineral money has created some
wealth and hence traffic jams, enhanced by a fairly lackadaisi-
cal approach to roadworks. The last thing we wanted arriving
after dark was to get stuck in one of them. But we did. And
with the GPS and the route book giving different directions

we had to rely on a GPS system that is really designed for sailors. It's brilliant in the desert but less so in urban areas where it tells you where you want to go but not how. We drove round our destinations in concentric circles, fortunately but not inevitably with diminishing radii. Eventually got there in what seemed the middle of the night. Fortunately dinner was available till midnight and we just made it...

DAY 5 (REST DAY)

The term 'rest day' is a misnomer. Mike has spent the entire day under the car and then had to make a trip to a welding shop to weld the chassis. As a result he missed the 'cocktail party'. He also missed the performance of traditional local music, so the evening wasn't a complete disaster for him! And he reckons the car is now in rather better shape than it was in Beijing.

He clearly managed to show a bit of discretion when talking to others because the Hickman/Gross blog for the day stated:

Doug and Mike McWilliams were making a new exhaust mounting bracket for their 1958 Bentley. They'd been having way too much fun over the last few days and whilst 'gently in the Bentley' is a good rule to live by, these guys seem to know what they're doing so can press on a bit when required and they are delighted with the way that the 'colonial spec' suspension soaks it all up.

I've done my best to help, doing minor chores during the day. We became millionaires in Mongolia after I changed a relatively small number of dollars to get local currency to pay for our fuel. Reminiscent of Italian lira pre the eurozone, or for the older generation (pre-1958) old French francs.

Ulaanbaatar is quite a sophisticated city given the general level of development of the country. The mineral wealth has spread around to some extent and there seems to be an urban middle class that has some of the trappings of modernity. I counted six coffee shops on the 700-metre walk to the car park. There is even a Bentley agent.

But its infrastructure lags behind. Roads are badly and slowly constructed. Roadworks seem to last for ever – certainly we have not seen anyone actually working on them. As a result traffic is a very slow-moving scrum, made more interesting by the Mongolian approach to queuing.

There clearly is a lot of mining. We passed a coal mine yesterday with about fifty Chinese lorries queued up to collect. The mining industry would be transformed by better infrastructure. On the other hand the desert, which is one of the world's major wildernesses, could be damaged. And the third of Mongolians who still practise a nomadic way of life might find that this does not easily mix with aggressive minerals exploitation.

Walking to the car this morning we passed a small demonstration. Mike reckoned it was about pollution and the environment. Considering why we were in the country, we decided to keep a low profile as we walked past.

The walk to the car took us past rather a lively sculpture of coloured camels. There are of course plenty of real ones around too, looking slightly more country coloured.

Mongolian men have a reputation for strength and it is not a surprise that their Olympic medals are in judo, wrestling, boxing and shooting. They are strong participants in the weightlifting divisions as well. Lord help us if they ever take up rugby. They look to be a race of front row forwards. Given the apparent solidity of the men, it is quite a surprise how petite many of the women look. There must be some genetic explanation but I can't quite work it out. All look well fed, even the nomadic people in the countryside who must have quite a hard life, particularly in the winter.

At 1,360 metres in altitude Ulaanbaatar is quite chilly even in midsummer. In the winter it is harsh – Mike tells me of a Malaysian friend who flew in one December and had to face temperatures of −35 degrees Celsius before returning to KL where the temperature was seventy degrees higher! Allegedly it is the coldest capital city in the world in winter.

Fortunately it is summer!

DAYS 6 TO 7

This morning we have to be on parade in the centre square of Ulaanbaatar at 8 a.m., which rather wrecks the advantage of our 11.05 a.m. start. Apparently we will beat the traffic by being taken there with a police escort. The mayor will make speeches and wave flags.

We are camping for the next four nights so are unlikely to post much unless (unlikely) we find a campsite with wifi!

We have traversed much of the Gobi Desert and against all expectations got to the Russian border. I gather that some of our organisers and fellow competitors have lost quite a lot of money shorting the distance we were likely to complete before we gave up.

No praise can be too high for Michael's car management and driving. And also the sweeps, who have fixed: a fuel tank with a hole the size of a foot in it (no they didn't try welding it!), brakes that wouldn't work, an exhaust pipe that had nearly fallen off, a car that was running on three cylinders and finally (again) the brakes which gave up completely last night. Some of the aluminium plates on the bottom of the car, after taking a fearsome pounding, have given up the ghost.

Mike drove 50 kilometres in the dark across the desert last night with no brakes at all. He had to stop once by reversing into a ditch so the back of the car doesn't look too pretty. Fortunately the colour of the duct tape nearly matches.

But we are still hanging in there and have got here under our own steam in line with a diminishing number of other competitors.

Those of us who have made it this far have become fatalistic. Either we will make it or not. Allegedly we have covered the most difficult bits. But dangerous to be complacent. And some of the car problems are cumulative so will continue to worsen if vibration takes its toll. Mike has been brilliant at the mechanical bits, working two to three hours most days.

DAY 8

Sorry that this account is all about the car. But that has become our major preoccupation.

The scenery is majestic. Camped by a beautiful lake, though sadly a lot of nature has chosen the same location. At times the insects have covered 50 per cent of any window. We climbed yesterday over a pass that peaked at 2,600 metres with stunning views, much better in real life than on the phone.

Mike 'fixed' the brakes last night, returning to the room around midnight. He and the poor sweeps, who have lost a quarter of their complement who are still rescuing people from Mongolia, worked their socks off.

Russia seems much more developed than I had expected, not that far behind emerging Eastern Europe or much of Southern Europe. While the border restrictions are mad, once in the country the high level of education of the people puts them in better shape than you might expect.

9

DAY 9 TO DAY 13: SIBERIA

DAYS 9 AND 10

Oh bliss. The car is working properly for the first time on the rally after the seven hours of work that Mike and the sweeps put in yesterday. The engine purred on its new spark plugs and it gave a huge amount of confidence to discover that the brakes worked. Until now we had ignored the fact that you can pick up penalties for arriving at a time control early. Today we actually picked one up, arriving twenty minutes early at one control point.

We are in Siberia. Sending people to Siberia used to be a form of punishment, started under the Tsars and pursued on an industrial scale by Stalin. Siberia in the winter must be 'interesting'. But Siberia in the summer is jawbreakingly beautiful.

It's rather like the best of Switzerland except there is just so much of it. We've been driving through this for most of three days now and it hasn't stopped.

Mike and I had expected Eastern Russia to be underdeveloped. But no. It is seriously sophisticated. Older people still live in the old ways but the young look just like people in the West, though a bit poorer. They look healthy and to have a decent diet. Most kids have at least a smattering of English. Tomorrow we reach Novosibirsk, the capital of Siberia and, after St Petersburg and Moscow, Russia's third city. Everyone gets their car rebuilt there on the rest day.

Russians are touchingly car mad. Everyone waves and when we stop people ask for autographs. Today we reached Novokuznetsk, which was (and still is) an industrial town based on steel production and coal mining. Ouch – suspect they are having economic problems...

One of the drivers on the rally (the one with the smart idea of doing the rally in a Lada) owns the hotel in which we are staying (the owner presumably has other cars...). It isn't at all bad, especially as the town is clearly not the most prosperous around.

DAYS 11 AND 12

But the rally is clearly something a bit special for the population of Novokuznetsk (and I doubt whether we would have stopped here had we not had a local on the rally). As I wrote this I could hear the strains of the town band practising for our send-off in a couple of hours' time – they carried on for the next two hours before rehearsal morphed directly into the real thing.

At last we have made it to Novosibirsk. Before the rally we were told that it is the dividing point of the rally. If you make it there, you get your car rebuilt by one of the numerous garages offering help and with luck you can make it till the end.

There is quite a lot to do on our car.

The front of the car is down on the driver's side and the wheel is at an odd angle, while the same side at the back is also low. Plus the problems with the brakes, the engine and the exhaust that I've been banging on about.

Since Mike's marathon at Lake Aya fixing the engine and the brakes, the car has run much better, though it still gets unhappy in heavy traffic or if it has to run for a long time at low revs.

But at least we are here. The hotel is swish, with attractive art deco features and comfortable rooms. Lots of those who dropped out at Ulaanbaatar or later have rejoined the rally here and we have welcomed them with a bit of a party atmosphere. But Mike and I again have been given separate rooms because some are missing. It's particularly useful to use the extra space for drying clothes after washing them.

After we arrived we went off for a curry with Nick and Dirk, who had just come back to the rally after crossing the border on a flatbed.

This morning Mike has gone off to sort out the car while I am left to write and catch up with the navigation plans.

Contrary to what I said yesterday morning, we saw some pretty impoverished villages on the drive in. Wood houses, corrugated iron roofs and only old people. Clearly there is a group left behind. And Novosibirsk, which claims to be Russia's third city, is in reality only seventh by GMP (Gross

Municipal Product – essentially equivalent to the Gross Value Added measurement which in turn is close to Gross Domestic Product – GDP – at a local level with some adjustment for taxation), with GDP per capita about half the Moscow level.[44]

Although people in Novosibirsk seem quite sophisticated, with an explosion of coffee shops, it is by no means rich and looks poorer than many places in the Far East. In particular it doesn't look as if a strong consumer economy has emerged and the shopping looks pretty desultory.

But again the young people look healthy and don't have the pockmarked faces that one tends to associate with a bad diet.

Given its geography, one suspects that this part of Russia will benefit most from the Belt and Road Initiative as it wends its way through Russia. There seems to be plenty of scope for upside!

DAY 13

We've had a pleasant stay in an upmarket Butlin's and now off to the rally again. Mike had a pretty busy day yesterday, getting the car fixed. We met the mechanic whom Russian-speaking sweep Nicolai had arranged for us at 9 a.m. (actually nearer 10 a.m., which is what passes for on time in these parts) and Mike and the car went off 5 kilometres to his garage. He returned thirteen hours later with the car in much better shape.

The car looks a lot better than yesterday, with the driver's side front wheel operating in the vertical plane.

Even the back of the car looks vaguely flat.

While Mike was getting the car cleaned I was doing more domestic chores. Fortunately I heeded the pre-rally warning not to use hotel laundries. There was a message from the hoteliers essentially saying that they had mixed up all our laundry.

Actually the Marriott in Novosibirsk isn't bad. But the high-pressure impact of the whole rally descending on a hotel can be overwhelming. I'm told that one year an ex-SAS man on the rally had to capture laundry that the hotel had grabbed using military tactics to befuddle the security.

We have a huge distance to go today – 620 kilometres and a border crossing. Because Russia and Kazakhstan have both been in the Eurasian Economic Union since 1 January 2015, we have been told that this border crossing should be relatively painless. Obviously our past experience warns against this. But (as we Brits are likely to find out) there may be consequences from being in an economic union with other countries! We'll learn more tomorrow…

Anyway, now I have to pack my washing and get going. Hope Mike is recovered from his hard day yesterday with no proper food (living on locusts and honey or the near equivalents). Will see him shortly for breakfast.

Wish us luck!

10

DAY 14 TO DAY 18: KAZAKHSTAN

DAYS 14 AND 15

I didn't manage to post an update yesterday – the hotel in Pavlodar didn't have working wifi, working air conditioning or indeed, at the time I went to bed, running water. The food was good though...

Quite apart from that it wasn't the very best day for most of us. We knew that the organisers had arranged that we do 620 kilometres on pretty rotten roads and then cross a border. What we didn't know was that they had also arranged a speed trial in a mudbath...

Keep your speed up to avoid getting stuck, we were warned. Interestingly the driver of an Alfa just ahead of us was warned not to push it too hard. They had obviously tailored the advice to their view of our individual driving styles and both of us in fact recorded exactly the same time to the nearest second. I had just handed over the driving to Mike, saying that this one looked as though it might need us both at our best (me navigating, him driving!). Mike in fact recorded one of the faster times as he drove through this field of mud, skidding and ploughing through, a surprising result for a car not exactly designed for the job. And had we not been held up by slower cars, only a few of which we were able to overtake, our time would have been much faster.

The mud did for some of the cars who arrived at the border on flatbeds. In between an entrepreneurial Siberian garage had organised a car wash. I saw it out of the corner of my eye and Mike managed a rapid two seventy degree turn into the garage. Ten dollars lighter we had a clean car... at least on the outside.

The border crossing into Kazakhstan confounded our expectations and took only twenty minutes. Kazakhstan, Russia, the Kyrgyz Republic and Belarus comprise the Eurasian Customs Union, which came into force on 1 January 2015. Obviously being part of a customs union has implications for border proceedings!

The Kazakhstan economy is based on oil and as a result petrol is cheap. A litre cost around 29p! We tweeted this on behalf of our good friends Howard Cox and Quentin Willson for whom Cebr have done some good work showing how high fuel prices harm economies. They deserve knighthoods for their sterling work campaigning (unpaid) for more sensible pricing.

The rest of the economy is heavily based on mining of various minerals and coal and as we drove the long straight road from Pavlodar to Nur-Sultan across the central Eurasian grasslands we passed quite a lot of examples. Hills made from mining spoils were a feature of the landscape. Mining is heavily dependent on transport infrastructure and it is no surprise that former Kazakh president (who still appears to lead the country as chairman of the country's Security Council) Nursultan Nazarbayev is a strong supporter of the Belt and Road Initiative. Cebr estimates that there will be a major impact on the Kazakh economy from this.[45]

Mike has actually worked here and knows the economy pretty well. He pointed out to me various geographical features and told me what they represented. In most cases they indicated mining – copper, gold and coal. We were pleased to drive on a long straight road which was in the process of being upgraded.

Eventually we reached Nur-Sultan. This is the Kazakh capital, renamed from Astana on 23 March 2019 following an apparently unanimous vote in the parliament. It was called Akmolinsk till 1961, Tselinograd till 1992, Akmola till 1997 and Astana till 2019, when it was renamed after the long-serving president 'not quite for life' Nursultan Nazarbayev. It is a bit reminiscent of Dubai and one senses that some of the architects and planners who have worked in the Emirates have also worked here.

Unusually we were greeted as we arrived at the hotel car park with a round of applause, as well as the more usual round of selfies and videos. And when we arrived at the hotel we were met with the news that a lady had been looking for us. I guess some ralliers might welcome such news with trepidation but both Mike and I had clear consciences so we investigated this further.

It turned out that the wife of the ambassador, who is a good friend of one of Ianthe's and my very close friends, Guy Gantley, had come to visit us with the economic secretary from the embassy and left some wonderful good luck cards and some chocolate. It was really appreciated because the day hadn't run exactly smoothly but we were hugely disappointed that after they had made such an effort we had been unable to meet them...

Our start had been delayed because the car wouldn't start. Half an hour under the car and some sterling work hitting the fuel pump with a hammer got it going, but halfway down the highway the fuel pump gave up completely. Fortunately Mike, whose planning for this expedition has been brilliant, had a spare one. With the help of the roadside support we replaced it in a couple of hours.

It took us 100 metres before the car stopped again. Lots of testing and phone calls to the sweeps and we tried putting a fuel lead into one of our spare jerrycans. We quickly discovered that far from sucking petrol from the jerrycan it was blowing bubbles into it... the pump had clearly been fitted the wrong way round! Another couple of hours later we were on our way, at a speed which discretion forbids us to disclose...

DAYS 16 TO 18

We left Nur-Sultan's fleshpots and pottered along to a wonderful welcome in Balkashino where we camped.

This is the last camping of the trip and was notable for thunderstorms which left everything boggy. It is possible that I will never camp again. Certainly not deliberately, though given my sensible political views I cannot rule out being sent to a labour camp if Corbyn gets in.

We had to cross a waist-high river to get into the camp. The local advice was to do it quickly which we did. Fortunately the car had taken the same advice and the engine kept going (as it did when we drove even faster through the same river to get out).

Two mini highlights: an Aussie 'lady' barging me out of a queue so that she could get the precise start time that she wanted at a time control. Since she was a lot taller than me I didn't challenge her. But some of those fighting for position are fiercely competitive! And a rather scenic picnic in a national park where we ate the chocolate that had kindly been donated the previous day.

The rally leader is still Gerry Crown, who has won twice previously. He is eighty-seven years old! Wow.

Everyone on the rally has nothing but praise for most Kazakh people. Everywhere we have arrived here we have been met with crowds and local festivities. They have treated us like heroes.

Unfortunately it is a bit intimidating when people thrust their kids in front of you to take selfies as you are trying to park. We have so much in the back of the car that there is no rear vision, our slow-motion braking system hardly works and the engine is prone to overheating in traffic. I doubt if the crowds understand the risks they are taking...

We've managed to avoid killing any children so far!

People thrust small gifts into your hands, they all try to grab you for selfies with them or with the car, they dress up, they provide bands and, for the organisers, fancy yurts.

The Kazakhs are if anything even more car mad than the Siberians. If you stop by the wayside, expect to be surrounded by crowds. Mostly very friendly and offering help including one guy who offered a 200-kilometre tow to what he still called 'Astana' for free when our fuel pump had gone (the going rate on a flatbed is $4 per kilometre). When there are problems they are more from lack of understanding than malice, like the lorry driver who got out of his truck to inspect our fuel pump with petrol dripping everywhere and proceeded to light a cigarette! He seemed quite miffed when I shooed him away...

We had another event-free day. There was a fabulous run round a short circuit called the Ski Run (probably a langlauf track in winter) organised for us by the Astana Motor Club. We managed a quite respectable time. We skipped the gravel sections and motored gently in to Kostanay.

On the way we passed many acres of wheat fields. Kazakhstan is the world's tenth largest wheat exporter and exported $1 billion of wheat last year to a range of countries. It used to be one of the main grain suppliers to Central Asia but now increasingly sells its produce to China. All this will be boosted by improved infrastructure. Other major exports are oil and gas, copper (Mike noticed a number of hills that looked to have been made by copper mine tailings) and 'radioactive materials'.

But while Nur-Sultan had been very consciously modernised, it is amusing (though less so for some of the perpetually outraged Americans on the rally) to stay in a hotel that clearly hasn't been changed since Soviet times.

The entrance was just sand that had not even been paved over but simply covered with some old carpets. There was a lady with an office by the staircase on each floor, presumably to stop people sneaking in! One lift for the whole hotel. Much of the building seemed to be unfinished which is why it is so surprising that it is so out of date... there were no facilities except rudimentary wifi.

The hotel did offer car parking and its website announces that 'receptionists of our hotel are flexible persons'.

But the rooms were at least huge and one of the ralliers found that he had SEVEN beds in his room (none comfortable).

Mike, who in his travels has stayed in quite a lot of hotels in out of the way places, says it is the norm for places like this. And I got a good night's sleep, which is the key test of any hotel.

We've changed time zone but it's not yet clear whether the organisers have caught up. So there is some confusion about what time we are meant to be doing things. Some are operating on the actual time, some on yesterday's 'rally time' (it is a convention on rallies that even when a time zone is crossed, for rally timing purposes you keep to the time zone that was operating at the beginning of the day).*

---

* At least this is what I said in the blog. But it turned out that I was wrong. This part of Kazakhstan is close to Russia, and the mobile phone coverage is from Russia, so the phones settle on Russian time. But the local time is still Kazakh time, which is an hour earlier. I discovered this when Mike phoned me the next morning to ask why I was not at breakfast!

11

DAY 19 TO DAY 26: BACK INTO RUSSIA

DAY 19

Today we head back into Russia with another border crossing. Let's hope it goes as well as the crossing into Kazakhstan.

One of the elements of entertainment on the rally is the way that some of the participants unwittingly reinforce prejudices about national stereotypes.

Some (important to note not all) of the Germans put their towels down on the parking spaces early in the morning, some of the Aussies are fiercely competitive (four out of the top seven), some of the Americans whinge about the hotels (mind you I do too, but in my blog only), some of the Italians wear what appear to be Gucci-designed smartly tailored overalls when working on their cars, while other Italians are wonderful with the local children and hand out child-sized T-shirts with Paris Peking printed on them. And the Brits mainly seem to keep the bar open late and just want to get to Paris in comfort...

Today was a relaxed day. The organisers tend to get nervous about border crossings because they take unpredictable amounts of time and mess up rally schedules. So they normally (but not always) give us a relatively easy day when we have to cross them. Particularly anything involving Russia.

But this time the gods were on our side and we had an easy passage in less than half an hour.

As I've mentioned before, Russia, Kazakhstan, Belarus and the Kyrgyz Republic make up the Eurasian Economic Union and this clearly helps reduce customs formalities. In Russia immigration is the responsibility of the FSB (former KGB) and is handled efficiently. Customs are a law unto themselves.

And the icing on the cake was a border guard lady who despite wearing military fatigues still managed to look extremely glamorous. She flashed a wonderful smile as she wished us bon voyage.

We actually had two border crossings in a day as later we passed from Asia into Europe when we crossed the Ural River in Magnitogorsk. This is an iron and steel centre, one of the biggest in the world by the side of a mountain made largely of the iron ore which gives the city its name. The city is reputed to have the worst air quality in the world but this did not appear to be the case when we arrived. Mind you the whole town seemed to be out to greet us which would have made it difficult for them to be doing the activities that create the pollution.

We got an even better reception than elsewhere. Requests for autographs, selfies, vids etc. Mainly the attraction is the car, not us. But pleasing nevertheless though the engine starts to overheat if we get stuck in traffic for any great period so we find it hard to stay stopped while everyone gets the selfie with the car that they want.

This part of Russia, like some of the outlying areas in Siberia, still looks very poor. But the infrastructure is good and improving. Obviously distance is the problem – we are a long way away from anywhere. But the scenery in the foothills of the Urals is breathtaking.

We are staying on Lake Bannoe in a Soviet-era set of workers' holiday flats. The flats are basic (apparently they are planning to install lifts... sometime) with polyester sheets but the place makes up in natural beauty for what it lacks in style. The lake is stunning. And as we are in the Urals, we are also in ski resort territory. Lake Bannoe is ranked number one in the Urals for snowboarding by the World Snowboard Guide, so sounds like a place to avoid in winter. And it has the best bouncy castle I've ever seen...

It is interesting how much of the Soviet era survives even forty years on. Modernisation clearly proceeds at an uneven pace. And some Soviet-era institutions were built to last. Our block of workers' holiday flats have floors made of concrete which would be quite hard to demolish (though the walls are another thing).

It's actually quite pleasing to see places that are quite wonderful being made available to those near the bottom of the pile in social terms. I guess these places will be spoiled when they get fully opened up to tourism and bought out by those who are better off but at present we are getting a special glimpse into some great places before they are ruined.

And fun to discover connections on the rally. Barry Nash runs a garage in Benenden close to Tenterden where Mike lives and where we are moving. One of the Italians is a fellow Cresta rider and a member of the St Moritz Tobogganing Club.

DAY 20

We had no serious mechanical problems today. The car was not charging properly in the morning so we (with the help of the sweeps who had the right spanners) tightened up the fan belt at the first stop which solved the problem.

Today we head off to Ufa for a stay in the Hilton and a rest day. Although the car is running reasonably well (touch wood, of which fortunately there is a lot in the car), it needs a thorough check-up and service to try to help it get to Paris.

And from the map it looks as though the drive takes us through some more stunning scenery as we traverse the mighty Urals.

We had a good drive across the Urals to Ufa. The day started with a trip to the local racing circuit where Mike surprised the organisers with one of the faster times. Since the Bentley isn't really designed for race circuits, it is a testament to his driving skills.

Then probably the most scenic drive so far through what could be the Alps except much longer and wider. The Urals really are beautiful, though (at least at their softer southern fringe) less rugged than the Alps and much less so than the Pyrenees.

DAY 21

Ufa is strangely unknown for a city of over a million inhabitants. It is the Muslim capital of Russia and the capital of Bashkortostan. The population is largely Bashkir and most road signs are in Bashkir as well as Russian. There are some splendid mosques including the as-yet-unfinished Ar-Rahim Mosque which dominates the city as you enter it from the south. It apparently has as a relic a hair from the Prophet's beard.

We booked a garage early and ended up being sent to the local Toyota dealership. The men there seem quite excited to be working on analogue rather than digital and seem to be doing a great job, though only made possible by Mike's planning – they didn't have brake hose but he had and didn't have a flaring tool but he also had. He also explained how you can only bleed the brakes with the car jacked up so the wheels are off the ground as they have to be turning for this to happen.

So Mike is in the garage getting the car fixed while I'm writing. Doesn't quite seem a fair division of labour...

Mike's artist wife Rowena* was inspired by the blog to paint her imagined scenes from the rally. I've included a picture of one of them which was inspired by Mike's

* Smallhythe Studios: www.smallhythestudio.com/

50-kilometre drive through the night in the desert in Mongolia with no brakes. It captures the uncertainty about where to go. Arguably it is easier to drive without brakes at night because at least you can't see what you are missing...

Today is a 'rest' day in the rally and we did actually get a chance to slow down a bit. Mike spent the morning at the Toyota dealer where the car had been left the previous night. I blogged and washed clothes.

The guys from the Toyota garage did us proud. Some of the younger mechanics had never seen some of the mechanisms on a car like an old Bentley and they often crowded round as Mike and the older mechanics revealed to them various mysteries like how drum brakes work. Mike's driving style makes rather less use of brakes than some, but I certainly prefer to have them working.

Not only do we have working brakes but also fresh rubber and new plugs. Various systems have been oiled and greased. The old tyres were by no means fully depreciated but have been relegated to acting as spares.

DAY 22 (REST DAY)

Lunchtime was spent with other rally crews catching up with their gossip. This mainly concerned the amount of support that some of the more aggressive crews have been using. Various non-rally mechanics have been flown in by about twenty of the richer crews, some of whom appear to be spending between £10 million and £15 million on the rally. Some of the crews apparently have vans travelling behind them to act as mechanical assistants. Others have had spares flown in. It becomes clear that we, by comparison, have been doing the rally on the cheap! We thought we had been flying at least business class but it turns out we are going easyJet!

Despite this we are officially in place fifty-two, though of those cars that have arrived here under their own steam without being towed or trailered we are about thirtieth (and last!).

In the evening we searched out local restaurants. The first we tried was booked for a private event. Then we discovered an Irish pub which to our great joy advertised their beer from East Lothian.

The Belhaven Brewery in Dunbar is just a few miles from our parents' home in East Lothian and it was good to see that their export drive takes their product as far as Ufa, though the locals clearly think it is Irish. We decided not to undermine the trade by disabusing the locals of this notion...

Enjoyed excellent burgers at the locally owned 'Prime Burger Gourmet'. Because of Ufa's position as a Bashkir city, where Bashkir is the second (and sometimes first) language, the proportion of English speakers is quite low and making yourself understood is a non-trivial task – fortunately the burger restaurant had pictures, which helped a lot.

We had a wander round the local market, making the occasional 'investment', and a walk back to the hotel above the banks of the local river.

Then back to our rooms. Mike downloaded his photos, many of which are pretty special and some of which are in this book, while I downloaded the latest Springsteen album. We will have music as we drive today to Kazan. Should be another day of great views and Kazan has a reputation for having a lot of sights including a famous Kremlin.

As we move west everything becomes more Europeanised. Mosques are replaced by cathedrals. Squat loos disappear (great news for those with bad knees). A much higher proportion of the population speak English.

We have driven from Ufa to Kazan. This was by far the worst day of the rally. My navigating was pretty awful and the brakes on the car seized up. Mike disconnected the brakes but by the time we got to Kazan neither of us were in the best of moods, Mike because of my bad navigating, me because he was refusing to take advice which if you are navigating is a real problem. We had a few beers in the evening which was probably not the most sensible thing to do, given our incendiary moods.

I spent most of the night sleeping in the car...

DAY 23

We are now in Nizhny Novgorod, rather a wonderful city. To some it's known as Russia's Detroit because cars, lorries and tanks were made here. But it has a great historic old town and some very beautiful buildings, including the Alexander Nevsky Cathedral, which dominates the view over the city.

The city is at the confluence of the Oka and Volga rivers and is now a popular destination for those cruising down the Volga. Because of its importance to the Russian military, foreigners were banned from the city in the Soviet era and only allowed back in 1991. It is also famous as the birthplace of the writer Maxim Gorky.

Perhaps because they have had to develop their tourist trade from zero, the civic authorities have put on a great show for us and made us very welcome. Mike has excelled himself at signing autographs while we have had to tolerate the imposition of hundreds (OK, more like tens!) of pretty girls insisting that they have their photos taken with us.

And our brakes have been playing up, making low-speed manoeuvring complicated, pretty frightening when people are lining up with prams, babies and small errant children all around us.

For a few days now we've occasionally found ourselves behind a 'Maigret' Citroën. And each time we've been a bit surprised at its turn of speed. It certainly didn't hold us up.

Eventually I said to Mike, 'I bet he's souped up the engine.' Little did we know that the car is driven by Mario Illien, founder of Ilmor and one of the greatest motor racing engine builders of all time, and his daughter Noele. Ilmor has won the F1 World Championship twice and succeeded at IndyCar racing, powerboat racing and even motorcycle racing. Eventually their F1 business was bought out by Mercedes and their engines are still dominating the sport.

Everyone on the rally likes Mario and Noele, for their modest demeanour, their refusal to accept additional backup and their insistence on doing their own work on the car.

PS Mike has returned from the Skoda garage (Skodas are now made in Nizhny, not only for the Russian market) with the brakes working. Fifteen mechanics worked on the car with him till 1.30 a.m., and not only refused to accept payment, but showered him with gifts...

Nizhny is a fascinating town that I hope to revisit. It is clearly an economic growth centre in Russia. It was the first area to privatise its small businesses in the early 1990s and has kept its lead. Its heavy industries also transformed. General Motors and Skoda moved in and it is now one of Skoda's top production centres worldwide. It is now also moving into a new generation of industry based on big data and tech.

Mike had a super time at the Skoda workshop while he got the brakes fixed. Because the mechanics didn't want him looking over them as they worked, the managers entertained him with stories including how during the war they built submarines there and transported them thousands of miles to the sea. Some of the other stories are too interesting to print...

The car park of the hotel has a many times life-size statue of Lenin that was still observing us as we left.

DAY 24

On our 690-kilometre journey we passed scores of churches – one begins to understand how Karl Marx's frustration led him to allege that 'religion is the opium of the masses'.

This was mainly a transit day and the driving was uneventful. We took a westward line about 100 kilometres north of Moscow.

Some observations on Russia. Past drivers on the rally commented on the risk from drunken drivers, especially in trucks. We've spoken to hundreds of truck drivers at cafes and petrol stations. Not one smelt of alcohol. Life expectancy has risen sharply in the past thirty years, by nearly six years for men. This may well reflect increased sobriety. Still, Russia has a twelve-year gap in life expectancy between men and women, the highest in the world.

Russian drivers seem much better at home than in St John's Wood High Street. Road manners are good. Although there are queue jumpers in traffic jams, it is not like Mongolia where it seems to be the national sport. In Russia nineteen out of twenty don't queue jump. Those who do, as in St John's Wood, seem to be in large 4x4s!

We finished the day in Zavidovo. This is a brand spanking new special economic zone for recreational pursuits and technology built around a lake. We watched water skiers being pulled by zip wire, and golfers in their buggies.

President Putin has a weekend retreat here. It looks pretty good, but a bit empty so far. Time will tell whether enterprise can overcome bureaucracy.

DAY 25

Today is the longest driving day of the rally as we drive to St Petersburg. I suspect mainly motorway, followed by the inevitable jam as we enter town. Fingers crossed for us and the car…

Another essentially transitory day though we had an interesting stop in Veliky Novgorod. This is one of the most important ancient cities in Russia. It was pretty well totally destroyed during the war but has been brilliantly rebuilt to become a UNESCO World Heritage Site in 1992.

This is one of the oldest towns in Russia and has an exotic history. It was attacked twenty-six times by the Swedes and eleven times by various German states. The Swedes last occupied it in 1611. It has an ancient Kremlin dating back to the fourteenth century containing the oldest palace in Russia. Although it wasn't a formal member of the Hanseatic

Filling up the Fair Fuel-supported Bentley in Kazakhstan with petrol costing 29p a litre.

The power station about 400km from Nur-Sultan is coal powered and what looks like steam is actually ash. The upgrading of the highway is a Belt and Road project.

The local band welcomed us in Balkashino…

The super yurt for the organisers' tent in Balkashino – normally the organisers' office is a desk in a field!

Two of the children we avoided running over in Balkashino camp...

For some reason the S1 was the centre of attention whenever we risked stopping. But it was a bit frightening with no low-speed braking and an engine always on the brink of overheating. This picture was taken in Magnitogorsk.

Happy campers in the workers' holiday camp. Alan (next to Mike) and his brother Steve Maden (opposite him) from Melbourne were in a Rolls-Royce Silver Shadow and saved our bacon by lending us fuel bladders to hold petrol. Barry Nash, behind Steve, owns a garage in Benenden and with Malcolm Lister (opposite) was driving a Rover 3.5 litre.

The Ar-Rahim Mosque in Ufa, which dominates the skyline as you enter the city from the south.

Moonlit madness – painting by Mike's wife Rowena inspired by the no-brakes moonlit drive in the desert.

We were delighted to discover beer in Ufa from Dunbar in East Lothian, even if the locals think it comes from Ireland.

The Alexander Nevsky Cathedral dominates the skyline in Nizhny Novgorod.

Parked under the baleful gaze of Lenin in Nizhny Novgorod.

The Kremlin at Veliky Novgorod, totally rebuilt after the war.

The unusual aspect of this picture, taken with one of the state lodges in St Petersburg in the background, is that I am working on the car while Mike is standing supervising. Mike had just brilliantly improvised a tool to reinstate a connecting spring on the brake on that wheel and I felt heavily in deficit on the manual labour side – so at least I replaced the wheel.

Some of St Petersburg's impressive new infrastructure.

Stalin's personal car, exhibited in Riga's car museum. It even has a stuffed dummy of the dictator in the back of the car.

Many of the roads in Poland exhibited these Hockneyesque features.

A characteristic scene in a hotel car park. Judging by the birch trees and the dead butterflies on the grill, it was probably taken in Siberia. Mike looks to be working on the plugs, which caused endless frustration. The car behind is Gerry Crown's Leyland P76, the winner of the event.

Mike and the sweeps fixing the car in Poland. This time a spare electrical lead was shorting the fuel pump.

For some reason the Germans think drivers should be warned against driving into trees.

The VW museum in Wolfsburg even has a Bentley, surprisingly similar to ours.

Lee Harman and Bill Ward celebrating 4 July in the VW museum.

We push the car into the Place Vendôme to stop it overheating in traffic.

Even the world's greatest ever F1 engine designer, Mario Illien (grey shorts and shirt), has to push his car into the Place Vendôme.

Mum and Dad greeting us at the finish line.

League it acted as the Eastern entrepôt for the league for trade with the states that became Russia, trading in furs and other Russian specialities.

The Kremlin is pretty huge though we had time to walk around part of it.

When we finally arrived in St Petersburg we discovered that we had hit the city during its famous 'White Nights', where it never actually gets dark partly because of the latitude but also because of light refracted off the atmosphere, which lasts from the beginning of June to mid-July. Both locals and visitors believe that everyone should spend at least one night awake all night revelling during the period. Bars stay open.

It is a time of all-night festivities and said to be romantic. One reason why this might be is that all the city's bridges are raised for sailing boats, so if you get stuck on the wrong bank you cannot get home...

Oddly they also celebrate with fireworks, which don't really work as well without the background of a dark night sky.

By coincidence we are spending a second successive stay next to one of President Putin's palaces.

The Konstantin Palace is one of St Petersburg's great palaces and has been restored for the benefit of the president. It is here that various summits have been held. There is quite tight security, though probably not as much so as would be the case had the prez been in residence.

DAY 26 (REST DAY)

Today I'm hoping to get to see it as I gather it is open to the public.

One of the things that we noticed as we moved towards St Petersburg was how Scandinavian the place starts to be, from the midnight sun to the trees in the forest. Road signs are now in English as well as Russian.

Tomorrow we leave Russia to get back into Western Europe as we arrive in Finland. Hopefully this will be the last complicated border crossing…

Rally 'rest days' are not normally proper days off work – cars have to be fettled and problems dealt with. We found that one of the brake shoe return springs had fallen off and was rattling around. Mike came up with a pretty innovative solution to getting the spring back on. Unusually I was able to help by performing the minor task of putting the tyre and wheel back on. We also found that the car didn't need much water and that the minor oil leak didn't seem to be getting worse (one car on the rally was needing 12 litres of oil a day – ours needs 1 litre every three days, which isn't much worse than normal).

In the afternoon I tried to get into the Konstantin Palace but my brief discussion in sign language with the non-English-speaking guards seemed to suggest that booked excursion tours were the only way in.

The hotel and the villas surrounding it are often used for international events and we had some amusing discussions about the extent to which listening and other devices were spying on us in our rooms and elsewhere.

The hotel was booked for a wedding and so no food was available and we had to get the concierge to sort out taxis to take us to a local restaurant. The food was actually quite good and there was a pretty realistic-looking stuffed bear at the front!

They've reversed the rally order. We have been at the end of the queue which was quite a problem during the difficult bits as it meant we were consistently having to arrive in the dark – a major penalty in places like Mongolia where navigation was difficult at the best of times. We are now able to arrive early. Of course, the advantages are less when it stays light late and the roads are fairly simple.

12

DAY 27 TO DAY 29:
OUT OF RUSSIA

DAY 27

We started relatively early on Friday because of the border crossing into Finland. We were both surprised by the extent of the infrastructural development around St Petersburg – we had expected hours of being stuck in traffic but instead were able to sail through at a decent speed on spanking new roads. There has clearly been an explosion of property development around St Petersburg and it gave the impression of great vibrancy.

It was a bit surprising to realise that after St Petersburg we still had 150 kilometres to go to get to the border.

The border area has been fought over frequently. In the peace treaty ending World War 2 Vyborg, previously Finland's second largest city, was ceded to Russia, though first the city had to be depopulated.

The border seems to be an area of tension, apparently because gangs are organising people smuggling. It actually took longer to get into Finland than to get out of Russia, which was a surprise.

Pleasant roads in Finland, some gravel but none potholed and a fairly peaceful drive. This is the second time we have stayed in a hotel owned by one of the participants and it is very pleasant. The Finns seem to love their classic cars and we had people waving and taking photos most of the way. The local rally clubs have turned out in force and in the car park at the hotel, there were nearly as many local classic cars as there were on the rally. We have been made very welcome.

And after the work we did on the rest day the car behaved itself all day! Fingers crossed it continues to do so...

DAY 28

We skipped the two rallycross sections of the route, carefully designed by the Finnish friends of the rally. We were sorry to let them down but when we discovered that at least one of the cars had ended in a ditch the decision seemed justified.

This gave us time to have a walk around Helsinki and see some of the key buildings. I liked St John's Church, which presumably in a more Episcopalian country would be the cathedral. The painted altarpiece was by Sibelius' brother-in-law.

Then we queued for the impressive Megastar ferry across to Tallinn. This was a revelation. For anyone used to ferry crossings across the Channel, it seemed so much better organised.

The ferry is brand spanking new and is LNG powered. Everything is properly clean. The shop is like a department store on three floors and obviously the non-Finnish prices for alcohol help subsidise the experience. Loading and unloading were managed clearly and quickly.

With a relatively light driving day and a restful ferry crossing, we had the chance to explore a second Baltic capital city in the evening.

The Estonians seem to have made the transition to capitalism fairly easily. They went through a painful period initially and the population declined from 1.6 million to 1.3 million, but the consequence has been rapid growth since. They have now joined the euro and have levels of real GDP per capita well above many parts of Southern Europe. The government has been very focused on boosting the tourist economy and is a world leader in adopting e-government (interestingly the Russians are playing quite a good game of catch-up here). But the financial crisis burst a bubble and GDP declined by a third. It has one of the lowest debt-to-GDP ratios in the world. Prices seem low by international standards which makes it seem attractive to tourists. A group of Estonians helped invent Skype, 44 per cent of whose employees are based around Tallinn. They even vote electronically and have done so since 2005.

Tallinn has become a bit of a mecca for stag dos, possibly because of the country's ratio of only eighty-four men per hundred women, allegedly the lowest in the world, and there were some traces of lively Brits and Scandis celebrating.

But we had a pleasant walk around the old city and avoided the temptation of the curry house in the main square. It's another place I'd like to revisit, possibly as a weekend break.

One place we avoided was the establishment opposite our hotel. The sign on it (Massaaz ja striptiis) suggested that there are some words in Estonian that translate fairly easily into English...

It's been a long rally and ralliers are starting to look tired. Someone had a birthday yesterday and was offering vodka shots en masse. I suspect those who accepted them to boost their short-term adrenalin will suffer today...

DAY 29

We had a beautiful drive, a lot of it down the coastline. I would guess that quite a lot of Latvians have holiday homes near the coast and this seems to be confirmed by my cursory online research. These tend to be fairly basic but provide all the facilities one needs for a summer seaside cottage.[46] There are long sandy beaches which on a hot day looked very inviting...

Before arriving in Riga we visited the capital's car museum on the outskirts, which is world renowned. Its collection is arranged by era, and each era is supported by videos of events of their time and relevant music.

Quite a lot of the cars on the rally were represented in some form in the museum and many of us looked enviously on the museum cars to see if they could have parts 'borrowed' from them. There was a rather beautiful Bentley that might well have had some useful suspension bits for us...

One of the highlights is the world's biggest collection of Russian ministerial cars, ZISs and ZILs. These huge armoured cars were heavily based on US cars of a few years earlier but with everything beefed up. They weigh four tons upwards, more than many trucks!

They even have Stalin's personal car with a stuffed dummy of him sitting in the back. All rather gruesome...

Riga itself is a beautiful city as we could see from our suite of rooms overlooking the river. But by the time we arrived, it was too hot to do much sightseeing so we contented ourselves with looking at the wonderful view.

The Latvian economy is interesting. Like Estonia, they privatised fast after independence but kept the utilities in state hands. Energy is largely by hydro power. Like other Baltic states, they had a wobble during the financial crisis, with a 19 per cent decline in GDP in 2009. But the economy is back on a growth path, based on financial services.

The latest IMF country visit reported just before we arrived. Their analysis supports the view taken in Cebr's World Economic League Table 2019 that growth would continue to outperform most of Europe, but would slow. Riga has quite a developed financial centre but there appear to be concerns about the extent to which it is used for money laundering.

Today we move on to Poland, where we spend three nights. The Polish Classic Car Rallying Club is promising great support, though we will have to avoid the rally tests if we want the car's brakes to last all the way to Paris...

13

DAY 30 TO DAY 33: THE SWEEPS' PARTY AND MOVING WEST

DAYS 30 AND 31

The most important social event of the rally is the 'sweeps' party'. The sweeps are special people. They're some of the top mechanics in the world, who come on the rally to pick up the stragglers. We would still be in Mongolia but for them. And not only can they fix cars but also they know how to party. The party is normally held at the tail end of the rally but car parking problems (the party has to be held in the sweeps' area, which is the car parks where they hold court) meant that it was held a week early. Their party was held last night.

So my text is trying to piece together the events of a couple of days!

On Monday we drove from Latvia through Lithuania and ended up in the Masurian Lakes in Poland.

Lithuania was notable for the fact that every village had speed bumps. I can't help but feel that this is correlated with the fact that they seem to be growing more slowly than the other Baltic states! This is obviously a controversial view but my experience tells me that places that show a dislike for cars tend to perform economically rather less well than those who find ways of managing them and the undoubted problems they impose on others.

The Masurian Lakes are of course famous for the two World War 1 battles and for their impact on World War 2, where Hitler's tanks had to be taken round the area rather than become bogged down which created a delay that may have contributed to his failure to conquer Russia before winter set in in 1941. This scene of so much history is now relegated to being a rather pleasant resort area with the lakes linked by canals for easy sailing. Mikolajki, where we stayed, is world famous for its international contest for singing sea shanties... apparently...

Poland is a much larger country than I think most of us in the UK realise. We spent part of Monday driving across, the whole of Tuesday and will spend Wednesday night in the country before reaching Germany.

The rally organisers have done us proud with beautiful tree-lined roads and interesting fields with sights like windmills.

Today (Tuesday) we had lunch in a town called Kwidzyn, pronounced Quids In. We went into what looked like a pretty unpromising pub mainly because we saw the French contingent going there. These guys can be guaranteed to find the best food anywhere.

Three harassed ladies who had probably never managed to serve more than fifteen customers at a time suddenly had to cope with a couple of hundred ralliers. The lady in charge was clearly at her wits' end – she couldn't remember who had ordered what or what she had given to us. Had she not been reminded she probably would have forgotten to charge us. We took pity on her and asked her for whatever was easiest. She said chicken and chips so we said yes, both of us expecting the worst.

And we had some of the best chicken and chips we had ever had! The chicken was clearly free range and had been fed on something interesting. The chips were proper and crisp on the outside and fully cooked on the inside.

In the circumstances it was most impressive. And with a couple of soft drinks it cost 50 zloties, equal to £10 – for two.

Tonight we are in Bydgoszcz. Awful car park and average hotel but a pretty decent feed as usual. According to the rally gossip, the event of the day was that the medics managed to run over someone. They haven't had a lot to do on this year's rally (they were partying late last night and claimed to have treated only a quarter of the number they expected) so we presume they are trying to create extra business...

DAY 32

We had had just about a week with no mechanical problems and had started to presume that getting to Paris was just a matter of filling up the car with petrol from time to time.

But it turned out that this was not to be the case.

About fifty miles into our route today from Bydgoszcz to Szczecin the engine suddenly died.

We had started unpacking the car to find our electrical spares, packed at the bottom because they were heavy, when Mike said, 'I have an idea.' And he changed a fuse. And the engine started.

So we repacked and drove on. For about 500 metres. And the engine died again. We changed the fuse again and it went for another while and the second fuse blew. So we put 30-amp fuse wire in and got a kilometre, just into the middle of a town square, when it died again, this time with a smell of burning and some blue smoke.

We phoned the sweeps. Meanwhile Mike changed the coil, which turned out not to be the problem. After we had unpacked again...

Eventually the sweeps arrived. We were lucky that one of them was Jack, who has owned a Bentley not that different from ours and who is often the man who can fix our problems.

It took him twenty minutes to work it out and twenty minutes to fix it. Pretty amazing.

In the UK we had put an extra wire to the fuel pump so we could keep going on the battery if the other electrics failed. This wire had moved and was now shorting the system.

The leads to the fuel pump were fried. Jack and Russ replaced them.

So we repacked and got on our way.

We missed time controls and lunch. And have dropped a place in the ranking.

But according to rumour, we are now one of only twenty-five cars out of the one hundred and six who started to have driven from the beginning to here in Szczecin under our own steam!

Szczecin has had an interesting history. It was of course the northern pole of Sir Winston Churchill's Iron Curtain: 'from Szczecin in the Baltic to Trieste in the Adriatic, an Iron Curtain has descended on Europe'. With Gdańsk it was one of the two founding places of Lech Walesa's revolt against Communism.

Today it is a rather calm and beautiful city, relaxing after so much turmoil. (Like us this evening after an eventful day.)

DAY 33

The settlement after World War 2 moved Szczecin from Germany to Poland. But the border with Germany is close by and we spent much of the day crossing what was East Germany.

In 1948 the population of East Germany was 20 million. Today it is a bit over 13 million, the same as in 1905. Because it is so depopulated, the fields seem to be used to a huge extent for solar panels and wind farms.

There still seems to be a huge cultural distance between Eastern and Western Germany though some gaps are narrowing.

Once we crossed the Elbe, which seems to mark the border between East and West, the difference, at least on the roads, was evident.

We ended up in Wolfsburg, home of VW. This was offered to the British motor industry after the war but they didn't want it...

They have built what is now the most visited auto museum in the world with 2 million annual visitors. Though the number is boosted by people who are waiting to collect their cars from the factory who get a free trip round the museum as a perk for saving on the delivery charge.

The town itself has been beautifully resorted and built up with boutique hotels and an attractive canal by the museum. The museum is a bit special with pavilions for each of the subsidiary companies under the VW holding company. One feature of the museum which makes it different from other motor museums set up by car companies is that it showcases cars made by other manufacturers. The Mercedes museum in Stuttgart is probably more comprehensive because of the extent of Mercedes involvement in different areas of the car industry but those cars in the VW museum are extremely well selected.

VW now own Bentley and the beautiful R-type Continental in the museum is in fact very similar under the skin to our own Bentley S1 which has travelled so far.

VW gave us a reception, the effect of which was slightly neutered by our need to drive and navigate a short distance further, so we drank alcohol-free beer.

Today is 4 July and our US friends have been enjoying themselves. We told them that Britain was not looking to repossess our former colony and that we wished them the best of luck with their independence. They dressed up in Independence outfits to mark the occasion.

We had a good day too. No car problems and some lovely driving roads. Looking forward to Paris and seeing our loved ones... only three days now, touch wood...

14

DAYS 34 AND 35: NEARLY THERE

DAY 34

Yesterday started badly when the car stuttered and the engine died at the exit barrier to the hotel car park. We pushed it out of the way and Mike changed the plugs. The front three as usual after we had been stuck in traffic were black. We got out of the car park and the engine died again. Suspected fuel pump problems and we were already using our spare.

We knew that the sweeps had some spare pumps and rushed back to the hotel to discover that the supply of spare pumps was already 200 kilometres down the road. I started phoning round garages in Wolfsburg to see if I could get one. The best prospect turned out to be in Florida, a firm called Wolfsburg Tuning based there, which I had dialled by mistake...

By now the sweeps had turned up and got to work. Eventually it turned out that the fuel supply from the tank to the engine was blocked and the pump was OK. The lead was unblocked but another fuel lead had managed also to get holed where it had been clamped.

Quite a lot of petrol had spilled when things got exciting... the local cops decided to take an interest. I was left to explain to them why they shouldn't have us towed away to the police pound while Mike and the sweeps kept working. Fortunately

Wolfsburg is a car town and the police, who were amazingly good natured, were satisfied with a name and address and a promise to pay for the cost of cleaning any mess. They even gave me a police badge!

But the drama wasn't over. Thirty kilometres further down the road the engine died again. Fortunately this happened when we were passing a motorway service station and Mike managed to freewheel across from the fast lane into the lorry park in the service area and the sweeps saw this fairly dramatic manoeuvre and followed us. This time we managed to get to the bottom of the problem. The makeshift repair to the fuel tank made in the Gobi Desert had eventually come unstuck and some tape had loosened and was blocking the fuel from getting out of the tank. A new makeshift repair using a bicycle tyre inner tube that had to be cut into rings was fashioned and we were on our way. By now we were many hours late and had to shortcut our route by taking the autobahn. (We subsequently discovered that we had picked up a speeding ticket when Mike was driving. A pic of the car and of Mike appeared in my post – the car is registered with me. Unusually the UK enables other EU countries to issue speeding tickets and to enforce them in the UK, something for which there appears not to be any reciprocity...

Germany seems to head for the hills after about 1 p.m. on a Friday afternoon so we spent most of the afternoon in motorway traffic jams. But we made it to the beautiful town of Liège and were rewarded with a Michelin-starred meal with Andrew and Charlotte, a super couple who make wine in Waiheke Island in New Zealand. A great end to a frustrating day. Not too much further to go...

DAY 35

We can't drive 'polluting' cars in Paris except on Sunday so the P2P organisers have in effect put us in a holding pattern north of the city. We spent the day running round small roads in Belgium following World War 1 battlefields.

In the morning we drove around the Namur area, in the afternoon round Ypres. The war cemeteries are a reminder of the tragedy of war.

We were given a 'free' lunch though presumably we had paid in some way as part of our rally fee. And ended up in a pretty awful hotel some way out of town.

But the car didn't break down. And tomorrow with luck we reach Paris.

15

DAY 36: ARRIVING IN PARIS

DAY 36

We were champing at the bit to get going on this, the last day. So it is hard in retrospect to work out why we waited until our official start time to get going. I think we had had a misleading impression of the extent to which our arrival in Paris had been organised and felt some obligation to fit in with the official timetable.

In fact our arrival had been disorganised for some reason and we all ended up taking pot luck and suffering huge delays as queues built up.

We hung around at the start and made conversation, all of us with half our brains concentrating on our arrival and our excitement at being reunited with friends and family.

Daniel Spadini, the best-dressed man on the rally, made the best joke – 'The rally must end today,' he assured me. I asked him why. 'Because I have run out of pressed shirts,' he responded. Somehow he caught the mood and we all relaxed a bit.

Eventually it was time to go. We meandered to the French border and then floated down various N roads to what we had expected to be some kind of a preliminary holding area. But clearly something had gone wrong.

Get to Paris in your own time, we were told. And so we set off for the Périphérique, the permanently jammed road that circles old Paris.

There we found traffic edging along at about 10 miles per hour but at least moving.

We had been meant to be held in a holding area just off the Périphérique but clearly something had gone wrong with this arrangement (we never quite found out what). So we carried straight on into the centre of Paris.

We navigated ourselves off at the appointed exit. There we were met by rollerskaters telling us in which direction we should go – though Paris is fairly easy to suss out. The traffic was building up, not helped by incessant roadworks. We decided to use bus lanes in the hope (so far justified) that we would not be prosecuted. Even with this minor illegality progress was glacial.

As we approached the Place Vendôme traffic ground to a halt. And as the engine temperature soared most of us turned off our engines and decided to push the cars the rest of the way. No point in ruining our engines by letting them overheat.

Obviously the news that we were close by had started to filter through to our friends. They started running out of the Place Vendôme to join us. By this stage we were out of the car pushing as friends handed us glasses of fizzy drinks or gins and tonics kindly brought by our sponsors. They joined us in pushing the car so it became a joint effort. It was such a thrill to see so many of our friends who had kindly come to Paris to celebrate our finishing. Thank God we did finish!

After taking nearly two hours to cover the last hundred metres, we arrived at the finish line. Thinking it would be undignified to be pushed over the line, we turned the engine back on and drove the last thirty metres. We were flagged in by the latest Prince Borghese who I think had been at university with my school friend Rikkee Curtis and who had initiated his (and indirectly my) interest in the rally. Tomas and Patrick from ERA were also present and congratulated us. But the greatest prize of all was to see family, especially our parents who in their nineties had stood for two hours in blazing sunshine to welcome us at the finish line. And of course our wives, Ianthe and Rowena, and Mike's son Chris, who with his partner Tamzin had been really kind in looking after the parents. Rowena had cut herself on a bollard in the square and in fact had needed medical attention but she disguised it well when we appeared and we only discovered later.

We had to park the car carefully because it was about the only vehicle in the rally not being transported back by Cars UK. We found a space that was not blocked and had the chance of celebrating with our generous friends including the sponsors Nicholson Gin who had turned up with both gin and tonic. We posed for photos and had a great time milking the moment.

Our movements were a bit complicated. We had to get the Bentley to our hotel, the Pavillon Henri IV in

Saint-Germain-en-Laye, get dressed in dinner jacket and long dress and return to the centre of Paris. Because of the traffic jams the schedule got tight. Mike kindly changed the plugs on the car for the last time to offset the damage from the previous two hours of waiting. I set off in the car, still using lanes that seemed reserved for other vehicles, and made my way. Fortunately the route was not too tight and once I found a bit of speed I found that even Parisian drivers gave me a wide berth.

Later that evening there was a ball and prize-giving, hosted by TV personality Steve Rider. I've never enjoyed these ceremonies, even when receiving a prize, and we all guessed that since Mike and I were not participating in the serious rallying, our achievements would be ignored. Which they were. The prize-giving ceremony didn't really work. We were held outside the dining room for nearly an hour with only water to drink, unlikely to improve the mood of ralliers who were all in need of something considerably stronger, and then the timetable got so far out of control that we were only served our main courses at 10 p.m. Endless speeches from organisers and prize recipients did little to improve our mood, though there was a very good film of the rally which managed to capture Mike in a characteristic position under the car. Eventually we wandered back to our hotel quite early.

But there was more to come. We felt quite strongly that those of our friends who had made the effort to join us deserved a party so we threw one for them the next day at our hotel in Saint-Germain-en-Laye. The hotel was in a lovely spot next to what had been the royal palace before Versailles and the palace that the French had provided for King James II (James VII of Scotland) when he had been forced into exile.

The Pavillon Henri IV itself had history, since Louis XIV, *le Roi Soleil*, had been born in the actual pavilion that today is the hotel. Placed on the escarpment beside the Saint-Germain-en-Laye gardens, it was the perfect location.

We had found it after a wonderful long research weekend in spring 2018 where we had gone testing restaurants to find a suitable location. I had decided that it would be difficult to find an appropriate space of sufficient size near the centre of Paris. Saint-Germain-en-Laye was actually, despite being some way out, highly accessible, about 200 metres from the RER stop. And although it was the last stop, the RER is sufficiently rapid that it takes very little time to get out there. Some of the other places that we had tested had food that was at least as good. But the location of the hotel clinched it. Ianthe had had some fun booking (with the help of her French teacher) and then sorting out the eating foibles and the inevitable changes in plans of our friends.

Guests started arriving at noon and the fun started. Ianthe had worked wonders arranging everyone carefully to be positioned near like-minded friends.

Mike and I both spoke. I think he spoke without notes. I decided not to take that risk. Below is a transcript of what I said:

'Welcome to all of you. Rowena, Ianthe, Mike and I are humbled that so many of you have come here; some even from different continents, like Barbara Bowie and Nancy Wrenn from the US and, from even further away, Stewart Labrooy from Malaysia. It's a little known fact that Stewart, Mike and I comprised the whole of a pop band when we were in our teens.

'The idea for going on this rally came after a very good family Christmas lunch in 2016. It was so good that when I suggested the idea, even Mike, who normally is the sensible one, said yes.

'The next issue was what car. In my mind there were three European cars from my period of choice, the 1950s, with the build quality to undertake the rally. Volvos, Mercedes and Rolls or Bentleys. And since I thought there would be lots of Volvos and Mercs and since when we were kids Dad used to drive S-series Bentleys, the Bentley it was.

'I'd like to share a few thoughts about the rally, which was probably the world's best geography lesson.

'There is a new Great Game taking place in Central Asia, a struggle for influence between the great powers. The name of the game is infrastructural development, which is transforming the region. At present I would say that China is winning, hands down.

'The second is Russia. Those who've been in Russia on the rally before were amazed at its transformation. Very few drunks, no visible gangsters and even petty crime was at least out of sight. Their life expectancy is shooting up and I'm sure their economy is doing much better than the figures suggest.

'The third is Mongolia. This country is set to change beyond recognition. But worth noting that the change has started. They have compulsory English language education and English is now the official second language. As the infrastructural improvements enable much more mineral extraction their way of life will change. I suspect they will be richer but not necessarily as happy.

'One of the most important lessons from the rally is that you can't get anything done without the help of others. Jeremy Padgett and his team rebuilt the car, which is an amazing machine. Sarah Conkay at Cebr helped Ianthe and me with a lot of the admin. The Cebr team, led by Graham, supported by Nina and Cristian, has coped with Mike's and my absence. Rowena and Ianthe put the sponsors' stickers on and dealt with a whole host of issues in Mike's and my absence. And Ianthe, with a bit of help from her French teacher, has organised this amazing lunch. Well done Ianthe.

'When our fuel tank was holed, two other competitors, Alan and Steve Maden and Lee Herman and Bill Ward gave us fuel canisters. Lee and Bill are with us today. Without them we would still be in Mongolia.

'May I please thank our sponsors. Our parents, Frank and Wyn, made a very generous financial contribution. Fair Fuel UK have done wonders campaigning for British motorists, thank you Howard for your support. Nicholson Gin have been brilliant and have kept us going on some of the rough patches. Fortunately their gin was too good to be used as a fuel additive in Mongolia. Our *good friend and board member Sin Chai from Inverlochy Castle also provided generous support.*

'But the real hero of the rally, who more or less single-handedly got us here, was Mike. Mike has nearly worn out his overalls working on the car. It was only three weeks into the rally that he let on that he'd also brought a pair of overalls for me... they remain unused. Mike planned the rally in such detail that all the other crews would come to us if they'd run out of things. Even the mechanics on the rally, the sweeps, admired his tools and borrowed them.

'And Mike drove the really difficult bits, I only drove the easy bits.

'Mike, you are one hell of a person, and I'm privileged to have you as a brother.

'Thanks for getting us here.'

Mike then gave a much better speech and hugged Rowena to great applause. Lee Harman kindly spoke up on behalf of our friends on the rally. And then a surprise – Dad stood up and gave a wonderful and kind speech where he spoke of his pride in his sons' achievement. We were just about in tears over that.

16

REFLECTIONS

It took us quite a while to get back down to earth. After the amazing lunch party on the Monday which Ianthe had organised we all worked our way back to the UK and tried to get on with our lives again.

We've kept in touch with quite a number of people from the rally either through social media or though meeting them personally. They will be friends for life. When you go through the sort of experiences that we went through on the rally there is a bond that will last.

Most of the participants with whom I've spoken since the rally ended, particularly the older ones, have told me how long it's taken to get back into a normal routine. Sleeping problems, a general feeling of lassitude and aching limbs have been amongst the symptoms reported.

I found the most difficult task was to come down from the adrenalin high and focus my attention on ordinary affairs.

The car was sent back to Mr Padgett who told us that the suspension was hanging on by only one bolt. A sobering thought. He made the car driveable and we took it back to show it off at the Bentley Concours d'Elegance at Blenheim Palace. This was a pretty swish occasion celebrating a hundred years of Bentleys. There was a black-tie dinner in the palace itself the night before and then a sunny garden party with 1,300 Bentleys. We were lucky enough to be joined by Jack Amies and his wonderful wife. Jack had done as much as anyone except Mike to keep the car going on the rally. Mark Seligman also joined us for a glass or two of gin. In all it was a wonderful event. But there was a slight whiff of the eve of the Russian Revolution about us Bentley owners having such a good time for ourselves in the grounds of a wonderful palace surrounded by such beautiful cars while so many people in the world are struggling to have a good life.

We even managed to show the car off on a second Sunday in a row. As we drove back from Blenheim we noticed an advert for a classic car show in Tenterden the following Sunday. I phoned up and the next thing we were invited. My parents and Ianthe joined us for what turned out to be an enjoyable day with a very impressive show.

On reflection we learned quite a lot from driving across the desert. We were probably overconfident when we set off and soon got taken down a peg when reality set in. I had certainly made much less of an effort than I should have to help Mike to prepare. Neither of us had realised how tough the rally would prove to be, although to be fair even experienced ralliers were surprised at the toughness of this one.

We learned a huge amount about the changing world of Eurasia by driving across it. The UK's tiff with its neighbours over Brexit seemed trivial and unimportant in the face of a world that was dramatically redefining itself and repositioning itself along the Russia–China axis.

Although some elements in the China economy look fragile, it would be surprising if it doesn't continue to power on, with political and economic influence continuing to grow hand in hand. The development of the Belt and Road Initiative will be critical.

But the biggest surprise was Russia. I had expected something more like Glasgow in the 1960s. Instead we saw a pretty modern state with updated infrastructure and the gangsters at least hidden from display. If you are worried about Russia, you should be even more worried, because they look to be combining their ambitions with competence. If you are more relaxed, it is a fascinating place and likely to play a growing role in the world, probably combined with China. What is clear is that the past dominance of the West has ended and we will have to live in the future with a very different world.

NOTES

1 *Rolls-Royce and Bentley Driver*, Issue 11, p. 55.
2 Richthofen, Ferdinand von (1877), 'Über die zentralasiatischen Seidenstrassen bis zum 2. Jh. n. Chr' [On the Central Asian Silk Roads until the 2nd century A.D.], *Verhandlungen der Gesellschaft für Erdkunde zu Berlin* (in German).
3 www.saltwoodkent.co.uk/alan-clark-s-bently-continental
4 Clark, Alan, *Backfire: A Passion for Cars and Motoring*, Weidenfeld & Nicholson, London, 2002.
5 Barzini, Luigi, *Peking to Paris: A Journey Across Two Continents in 1907*, Penguin Travel Library Paperback – 26 Jun 1986.
6 Duducu, Jem, *The Romans in 100 Facts*, Amberley Publishing, Stroud, 2015.
7 Grant, Michael, *History of Rome*, Charles Scribner, New York, 1978, p. 264.
8 These techniques are best described in the project reports of two European Commission-funded studies, ASTRA and UPTUN. The ASTRA project is written up at www.astra-model.eu/doc/ASTRA-model.pdf. The key data is on pages 28–41. The evaluation module of the UPTUN project is written up in Khoury, G.A., Walley, D. and McWilliams, D., 'New methods for road tunnel fire safety evaluation and upgrading', Proceedings of the Institution of Civil Engineers – Structures and Buildings, 162: 3, June 2009, pp. 183–197.
9 This work is described in Singham, Shanker and Niculescu-Marcu, Cristian: https://cebr.com/reports/us-china-brexit-its-all-about-international-trade-but-we-have-to-oil-the-wheels-at-home-too-domestic-and-export-markets-should-not-be-seen-as-separate/
10 'Belt and Road Initiative', World Bank, Washington March 2018.
11 Kuo, Lily and Kommenda, Niko, 'What is China's Belt and Road Initiative?' *The Guardian* (2018-09-05).
12 This term was taken from a book by Huntington, Samuel P., *Clash of Civilizations and the Remaking of World Order*, Simon and Schuster, New York, 1996.
13 Jay, Peter, *The Wealth of Man*, Public Affairs, 2000.
14 This is essentially the view of Max Weber in his path-breaking book Weber, Max, *The Protestant Ethic and the Spirit of Capitalism*, Penguin Books, reprinted 2002.

15 See my last but one book, *The Flat White Economy*, Duckworth, 2016.
16 Kroker, Molly, 'The "Great Divergence" Redefined: the Rise and Fall of the West and the Recovery of China', *Inquiries Journal*, 6: 9, 2014, www.inquiriesjournal.com/articles/917/3/the-great-divergence-redefined-the-rise-and-fall-of-the-west-and-the-recovery-of-china
17 For a fuller explanation of this, read Herman, Arthur, *How the Scots Invented the Modern World*, Crown Publishing Group, November 2001.
18 See the recent biography of Telford: Glover, Julian, *Man of Iron*, Bloomsbury, 2017.
19 https://press.princeton.edu/titles/10831.html
20 There are two main series for this: Feinstein, C., 'Changes in Nominal Wages, the Cost of Living, and Real Wages in the United Kingdom over Two Centuries, 1780–1990', in P. Scholliers and V. Zamagni (eds), *Labour's Reward*, Edward Elgar, Aldershot, Hants, 1995, pp. 3–36, 258–266; and Lindert, P.H. and Williamson, J.G., 'English Workers' Living Standards During the Industrial Revolution: A New Look', *Economic History Review* 36, 1983, pp. 1–25. Both are described well in Allen, Robert C., 'The Great Divergence in European Wages and Prices from the Middle Ages to the First World War', *Explorations in Economic History* 38, 2001, pp. 411–447.
21 Groningen Growth and Development Centre, Faculty of Economics and Business, Groningen University, www.rug.nl/ggdc/historicaldevelopment/ (in 1990 Geary–Khamis Dollars).
22 Ravallion, Martin, 'Ethnic Inequality and Poverty in Malaysia', paper written at the University of Malaya and available at: www.ecineq.org/ecineq_paris19/papers_EcineqPSE/paper_406.pdf
23 The only study that I can find in the academic literature that even considers this issue is Park, Keunho and Kawasakiya Clayton, Hiroko, 'The Vietnam War and the "Miracle of East Asia"', *Inter-Asia Cultural Studies*, 4: 3, 2003, pp. 372–398, which points out that it is traditional for economic development studies 'to search for general theories of economic development… accidental factors, including the Vietnam War, should be abstracted from economic development'.
24 Daggett, Stephen, 'Costs of Major US Wars', Congressional Research Service 7-5700, 29 June 2010, www.crs.gov RS22926.
25 McWilliams, D.F., 'Offshore Manufacturing in a Developing Country: A Malaysian Case Study', Lincoln College Oxford, unpublished MPhil thesis, 1974.
26 The key data on this for all the advanced countries is given in OECD Revenue Statistics. The latest issue is for 2018 and the relevant data showing the share of corporate taxes is given in Table 1 on page 3. It can be seen that only in Chile and Mexico is the share of tax paid

directly by corporates as much as a fifth of total tax – the remaining tax is paid by individuals.

27 My fellow Gresham Professor, Sir Richard Evans, has written eloquently about this; see www.gresham.ac.uk/series/the-rise-and-fall-of-european-empires-from-the-16th-to-the-20th-century/ for his views on the subject.

28 Figures from WHO see: https://www.worldlifeexpectancy.com/russia-life-expectancy

29 'Peking to Paris Rally Briton Killed in Siberia Car Crash', BBC News (13 June 2013), www.bbc.co.uk/news/uk-22885146

30 https://worldtop20.org/education-data-base?gclid=Cj0KCQjwjOrtBRC cARIsAEq4rW5o8VGxKM_mwO0vKAa5iStJckwO6g0ntrUr3VWR4 Dewhx-95f4kvNkaAug3EALw_wcB

31 IMF, 'Measuring the Digital Economy', 5 April 2018, p. 29.

32 See for example this study: www.dailywire.com/news/462-financial-journalists-were-asked-their-ashe-schow

33 www.nytimes.com/2019/07/17/sports/autoracing/peking-paris-race-motorcar.html

34 www.chinadaily.com.cn/a/201905/26/WS5cea60a7a3104842260bdcfd.html

35 I would highly recommend Joyce to anyone wanting guiding in Beijing – contact her through Catherine Lu Tours: book@catherinelutours.com

36 To read more see www.forbes.com/sites/tychodefeijter/2016/05/26/meet-the-hongqi-l5-chinas-most-expensive-car/#294c0b8658c7

37 Madison Project Database, Groningen University, 2013 release.

38 www.stlouisfed.org/on-the-economy/2018/january/income-living-standards-china

39 www.autoevolution.com/news/the-longest-traffic-jam-in-history-12-days-62-mile-long-47237.html

40 www.asiatimes.com/2019/03/article/beijing-home-prices-fall-10-over-two-years/

41 https://cebr.com/welt-2019/

42 https://cebr.com/welt-2019/

43 https://cebr.com/reports/belt-and-road-initiative-to-boost-world-gdp-by-over-7-trillion-per-annum-by-2040/

44 http://www.urbaneconomics.ru/en/MetropolitanRankingIUE2017

45 See https://cebr.com/reports/belt-and-road-initiative-to-boost-world-gdp-by-over-7-trillion-per-annum-by-2040/

46 e.g. see Raagmaa, Garri and Stead, Dominic (eds), *Impacts of European Territorial Policies in the Baltic States*, Routledge, London, 2015.

INDEX